TO:

____

FROM:

____

DATE:

____

Visit Christian Art Gifts website at www.christianartgifts.com.

101 Prayers for Military Wives

Published by Christian Art Gifts Inc., IL, USA

Designed by Allison Sowers

Author's photo by Laurie Garrison

Images used under license from Shutterstock.com

ISBN 978-1-64272-919-1

Printed in China

28 27 26 25 24 23
10 9 8 7 6 5 4 3 2 1

101 Prayers for Military Wives

KRISTI WOODS

DEDICATION

To the women whose hands hold this book,
stay the course.
Our faithful God stands at the helm.

★

INTRODUCTION

Dear Brave One,

That unseen uniform you wear requires courage, patience, hope, love, wisdom, and a God-sized heap of faith. You wear it well, yes, even when the threads of life feel like they're fraying. We serve the true life mender in this journey, God, and He remains steadfast regardless of how untucked or torn we feel.

Praise Him. Society tags military wives as strong and unbreakable. As the wife of a now retired United States Navy sailor, I bought into that weight-crushing fallacy. Susceptibility finds Christians, too—make no mistake. Its squawk sounded in my ear as I attempted to navigate the milspouse's journey. The plastic façade of self-sufficiency offered no respite. I cried, literally, over my son's spilled milk. Again. And nearly crumbled as shame, depression, exhaustion, and defeat whacked at my mental, emotional, spiritual, and physical stability.

But God. The dire need for our loving Father in those trenches became apparent and especially now as I reflect on those days. As women on installations across the globe navigating daily life with the uncertainties of the military lifestyle, we spouses face many challenges, but we're armed with something more powerful: the weapons of our warfare. With the love and strength that comes from above and amid cries for help that He hears, we find stamina and joy for the journey.

So friend, take these prayers and orient the terms to your husband's branch of service. Whether in gut-wrenching cries or with even-keeled tones, call out for help from above. Spend time, one-on-one, with the Father who loves you. He hears, He answers, and He leads victoriously.

To God be the glory,

Kristi

"Never be afraid
to trust
an unknown
future to
a known God."

Corrie ten Boom

PEACE AMID CHANGE

"Do not be anxious about anything,
but in every situation, by prayer and petition,
with thanksgiving, present your requests to God."

Philippians 4:6

Lord,

You know my thoughts and how they spin with anxiety when I face change. Relocations are hard! The *what-ifs* toss around their Goliath-like threats. *What if you don't like the orders? What if your family doesn't handle the news well? What if the move is a disaster?* I listen, clinging to the badgering whispers as if they are true. But it only causes me to stew—often to the detriment of relationships and my witness for You.

Forgive me for eating from anxiety's buffet. I crave, instead, the delicacy of Your counsel and peace. Strengthen me to refuse anxious thoughts whenever I'm tempted to chew on them. Whether it's the housing waitlist, dealing with the mountain of boxes, or the smallest need, cause me to savor Your truth and protection. Help me formulate simple yet profound prayers and petitions that flow freely from my lips. Settle me with a reminder to top them regularly with thanksgiving. No doubt You are deserving.

Thank You, faithful God, for guarding my heart and mind with Your beautiful peace.

Amen.

MY WORTH

"Even the very hairs of your head are all numbered.
So don't be afraid; you are worth more than many sparrows."

Matthew 10:30-31

★

Lord,

Hurt pricks at my heart when I don't feel valued—when people acknowledge my husband's service but fail to notice mine. When he's away, there's still a household to run, cars to take care of, and kids to single-handedly parent while juggling two people's responsibilities. You hear me question whether anyone cares. My self-will itches for someone's assurance, yet the void remains. Why do I continue to seek affirmation from others and not You, the true filler of my need? Help me, Lord.

My worth doesn't hinge on the notice or accolades of people, but it's found in You. You are worthy to be magnified. With the power of Your love, cast aside my fear of being unnoticed or disvalued. The fact that You care enough to number every hair on my head astounds me. Plant deep within me trust for Your truth, not man's opinion. Spur me to keep Your proclamations concerning me at the forefront of my thoughts, so they'll never be buried again. Glory to You, God.

Amen.

I WILL REJOICE

"Though the fig tree does not bud and there are no grapes on the vines, though the olive crop fails and the fields produce no food, though there are no sheep in the pen and no cattle in the stalls, yet I will rejoice in the LORD, I will be joyful in God my Savior."

Habakkuk 3:17-18

★

Lord,

Sometimes, I wrestle with discouragement. Plans change without warning, distance tears me from loved ones on holidays, or advancement eludes my husband—again. My thoughts camp with what's wrong versus the long list of all that's right. Disappointment is king, or so it seems. But then You remind me of Job and Habakkuk. Of the many who've faced trials yet rejoiced in You. And I know it doesn't have to be this way.

Instead, I will rejoice in You. Remove the heaviness cloaking me, Lord. Place words of celebration on my tongue, a fire that burns away despair. May praise blaze like an inferno, regardless of life's peaks and valleys. Impress upon my heart daily reminders of Your love and faithfulness. I don't want to forget or turn a blind eye to Your goodness. From now on, I will rejoice in You.

Amen.

WHEN I'M AFRAID

"I sought the LORD, and he answered me;
he delivered me from all my fears."

Psalm 34:4

Lord,

You know there are times when my mind races with fearful possibilities. I wonder about my husband's safety, whether our marriage can survive this time apart, or if we'll have enough money at the end of the month. My imagination gains ground, tossing around bad outcomes, and my insides knot. The scenarios play on an endless reel, toying with my sanity. Why am I placing my trust in these unlikely outcomes when my true deliverance is found in You?

Deliver me, Lord, from fear and the stories it authors. Sweep aside these pesky thoughts that lead to worthless or dangerous paths. Dismantle the lies with Your perfect love (1 John 4:18). Regardless of what I face, I desire to stand firm with courage and a mind that replays how all things are possible with You (Matthew 19:26). Cause me to focus on what's true, admirable, and praiseworthy (Philippians 4:8), finding delight there. If fear spouts its threats again and I'm tempted to believe the lies, draw me with truth. Pull me close and wrap me in Your peace, for You alone are my deliverer.

Amen.

HELP'S HERE

"When pride comes, then comes disgrace,
but with humility comes wisdom."

Proverbs 11:2

Lord,

I've bought into the notion that military wives are strong—that they handle on one pinky finger the difficulties of life. That they can do it all and never falter. I've believed the lie that every other military wife stands strong, and I must too. You've watched me shoulder the load alone. You know the thoughts that propel me to this, that I don't want to be the only weak-kneed military wife in history. But inside, I'm crumbling. I need You. I can't do this alone.

Save me from this weight of pride, heavenly Father. Loosen and remove its chain. No doubt You are my true help. And You cross my path with friends, fellow military wives, sisters and brothers in Christ, and others. Weave within this heart of mine a willingness to ask for and accept help from You and them. Embolden me to link arms not with fear, but with the wisdom that comes from Your Holy Spirit.

Amen.

“I know that you
can do all things;
no purpose of yours
can be thwarted.”

Job 42:2

PRAYING FOR MY HUSBAND

"Do not be like them, for your Father knows what you need before you ask him."

Matthew 6:8

Lord,

I'm struggling to find the words to pray for my husband. With distance between us and communication lacking, how do I know what to pray? Thoughts tumble around inside of me, but they feel disconnected, dry, and worthless. You listen as I rattle off a trailing list, hoping it hits the mark yet sensing a pang of insufficiency. Other times, the words refuse to come together and a void remains. I question their value, yet You call me to a life of trust and prayer.

Your Word assures me that You know my husband and his every need, whether he stands beside me or miles separate us. Confidence rises when I meditate on Your love for him and when I consider that only You truly know the heart. Settle on my lips the words to pray as I battle spiritually on his behalf, Father. Fill my thoughts with holy wisdom, and help me pinpoint requests. You guide my words with boldness and confidence, leading me on a straight path, as I petition for him. I trust in You, and You remain faithful.

Amen.

LOOKING PAST THE OUTSIDE

"But the LORD said to Samuel, 'Do not consider his appearance or his height, for I have rejected him. The LORD does not look at the things people look at. People look at the outward appearance, but the LORD looks at the heart.'"

1 Samuel 16:7

Lord,

Assumptions tangle me. I cling to my first impressions of people, failing to run them under love's magnifying glass. I jump to conclusions about new neighbors, people at the command, strangers, and even my husband. My focus lands on their looks, actions, and rank, categorizing according to what I see, but I fail to inquire about Your thoughts and ways for them. Yet, You see it all. Please forgive me for this. Snap me out of this shortsighted stare.

You give true vision. You cause me to discern beyond the external to the internal. Circle my thoughts and reactions around the heart, not what I notice on the outside. You focus my vision in ways far beyond my ability. Settle within me a righteous understanding of people's potential. Remind me of their true worth and Your glorious plans. Prod me to look deeper. To notice. And to celebrate Your praiseworthy craftmanship in them.

Amen.

SEARCH MY HEART

"I the LORD search the heart and examine the mind,
to reward each person according to their conduct,
according to what their deeds deserve."

Jeremiah 17:10

Lord,

When hard conversations happen, I jump to conclusions, especially with my husband. You watch as I make judgments about his intentions—certain I know full well the motive for his actions and words without truly listening. Most of the time, though, my interpretation lands far short of the truth, and it opens the door to trouble. I suspect I have a heart issue. Help me squelch these fast and hard assumptions. Help my heart.

You made my husband, and only You know the thoughts congregating inside of him—those on the surface and others deep within the heart. Not me. Forgive me, almighty God, for the swift judgments I've entertained, the conclusions I've jumped to. Search my heart. Uncover the lies. Wipe clean the dark smears. Draw me with truth, and unearth these assumptions when they attempt to seed. Open my ears that I might hear well. Embolden me to cast down musings with discernment from above, relying fully on Your understanding.

Praise Your holy name. Thank You for leading me triumphantly.

Amen.

A DECISION TO TRUST

"Trust in the LORD with all your heart
and lean not on your own understanding."

Proverbs 3:5

Lord,

Many options face my husband and me concerning new orders. East coast, west coast, overseas—which choice do we make? Shall we list our preferences without consulting You, snagging what seemingly fulfills our needs? We've traveled that path in the past, running down the pothole-filled trail paved with our own understanding. I cringe at the thought of handling this move in the same, dangerous way. Instead, I desire to place this decision in Your hands, so I run to You. Help my husband and me lean on Your understanding to make wise choices.

You assure me of Your trustworthiness. I believe You. Open wide my heart to fully trust You, Lord. Quiet my understanding, and bring rise to Yours. Whether or not circumstances, options, or outcomes make sense, I wring my hands of control. You are my strength and shield, the one who refuses to forsake me. You straighten my path because I acknowledge You (Proverbs 3:6). Faithful Father, take this choice my husband and I face, and make it Yours. Thank You for guiding us in love and with unfathomable wisdom.

Amen.

WHEN I'M SCARED

"Peace I leave with you; my peace I give you.
I do not give to you as the world gives. Do not let
your hearts be troubled and do not be afraid."

John 14:27

★

Lord,

My ear turns toward the news of war and difficulty. Thoughts of my husband come to mind, and fear grips me. I come undone as worry rips through me. This mental tug-of-war wears me thin. It attempts to conquer the truth of Your Word. No doubt, this life as a military wife isn't always easy, but You faithfully lead me always. Remind me and reassure me in these difficult times.

Forgive me for taking in what the world dishes out and for tuning in when I should tune out. Immerse me in Your peace. Take me into that quiet place of communion with You, a space where faithfulness paints the walls of my mind. Surround and protect my heart, purging it of the angst, worry, and anxiety. Your love coats me, casting aside the taunting fear. So, I will remember Your salvation and the power it wields. Nothing else compares to You, Jesus.

Thank You for reassuring me with Your peace.

Amen.

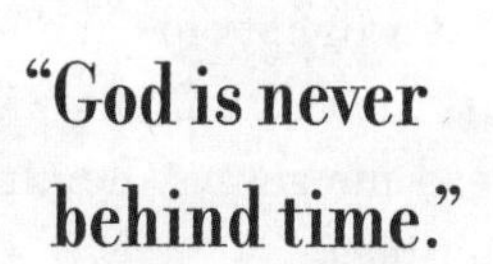

Mary Slessor

FINDING CONTENTEDNESS

"Keep your lives free from the love of money and be content with what you have, because God has said, 'Never will I leave you; never will I forsake you.'"

Hebrews 13:5

Lord,

The lure of owning and enjoying nice things tempts me. Social media paints its picture-perfect life. So do magazines, television, and even neighbors. Magazine-ready homes, must-have designer clothes and bags, and makeup products that promise to awaken my inner model—they capture my eye, causing me to toy with the idea that maybe my life and things don't measure up after all. You see the discontentment that seeds in my heart. It sprouts then grows. But no more. I hear the warning to uproot this temptation.

Embolden me to sever ties with those mingling feelings of want and desire. Muffle the world's restless whispers concerning gratification with salvation's hope. I cling to contentedness, for You're the supplier of all good things. Forget serving two masters (Luke 16:13). I won't. Instead, I choose You, for only You, Father, truly fill my deep vat of needs. You cause my heart to overflow with gratitude and satisfy my needs fully. Thank You for waiting on me, for not forsaking me.

Amen.

GOODBYE, GOOD GIRL

"Not by works, so that no one can boast."

Ephesians 2:9

Lord,

I love You and desire to walk in Your ways all the days of my life. Today, I feel You calling me to a deeper faith, but I've realized this need to "be good" creates a barrier. I question whether the schedule packed full of good opportunities—some even church-based—fill my flesh or are godly obedience. Good and godly don't always equate, do they? Why is this inner need fueling me versus a push to glorify You? Peel away the layers, Lord, leaving the truth laid bare.

Strip me of busy, self-fulfilling works, loving Father. Pride as well. Lead me away from my own understanding and good intentions. Draw me into the embrace of Your glorious grace. Assist me in differentiating between Your path and my own. Remind me that faith builds not by works, but by my Savior's loving sacrifice—Your free gift to me and something my works will never match. Your sufficient grace causes me to reject pride and walk with a humble spirit and to kick the good girl syndrome to the curb. And I'm grateful, almighty God. Praise You.

Amen.

GOD'S APPROVAL VERSUS MAN'S

"Fear of man will prove to be a snare,
but whoever trusts in the LORD is kept safe."

Proverbs 29:25

Lord,

Why do I care what others think about me? It tugs at me—this need to gain their approval and to look good in the eyes of neighbors, friends, and family. I'm enticed to make decisions hinging on people's approval, and it's tiring. Activities, group involvement, conversations—the temptation lingers. But what about You? Shouldn't I care more about Your thoughts? I want to fear You—to live in awe and worship, not scramble for Sister Suzie's approval. Help me shirk this foolish thinking, Holy One.

Strip me of selfishness and of this snare for man's approval. Clip the longings for others' acceptance, whether in the neighborhood, with friends, or even at church. Fill me, instead, with a longing to honor You, for Your love woos me. Your sufficient grace keeps me. Your faithfulness causes me to trust. You send me out to the world to proclaim Your glory, to worship, and to shine a light for the sake of Jesus. And I'm in awe of You, faithful God. Thank You for loving me. I will trust in You.

Amen.

HELP ME TO FORGIVE

"Be kind and compassionate to one another,
forgiving each other, just as in Christ God forgave you."

Ephesians 4:32

Lord,

You know the times when I hold on to hurt and struggle to forgive. I rehash those conversations. I stew about my husband's curt words or those of others. In my woundedness, I'm tempted to shake a finger and place ownership of the problem in the offender's court. I hold onto the hurt, feeling justified. Yet, I sin too. You forgave my many wrongs, and I know I should forgive, but something holds me back. Why do I struggle to offer those simple words "I forgive you"?

Take this heart of mine and soften it. Sand those hard edges with the grit of Your love. Shape me in Your likeness. Help me quiet the self-will that longs to protect itself and instead look past the hurtful words and remember the cross. Steel me to follow in Your ways, regardless of the direction my feelings attempt to take me, and to offer forgiveness aligned with generous and righteous motives.

Thank You for weaving grace and reconciliation into the fabric of my life. Your forgiveness humbles me and provides hope.

Amen.

BEING KIND

"Therefore, as God's chosen people, holy and dearly loved, clothe yourselves with compassion, kindness, humility, gentleness and patience."

Colossians 3:12

Lord,

When my neighbor's ways clash with mine, kindness sometimes takes a back seat. Squeezed into a small space with lives overlapping, I squirm with unease when our actions rub each other raw. My mind knows I should be kind, but my response takes a different tone. Whether face-to-face or in the quiet of my own thoughts, I choose the easy route paved with harsh impatience, rudeness, and an uncaring attitude. But this chips away at me. Instead, You've called me to the narrow way—to embrace and share patience and kindness.

Forgive me for my hard-edged attitude, Lord. Soften my hardened heart. You wipe clean the thoughts and spoken words to which I've given permission. Loosen this stiff neck of mine; cause it to flow with righteous deeds and kind words. You break my stubborn and selfish attitude, taking this heart of mine and restoring it with gentleness, grace, and love. Wash me with tenderness as I, in an act of worship to You, willingly clothe myself with kindness and patience and bear the fruit of Your Spirit.

Thank You, Father.

Amen

Jesus looked at them and said, "With man this is impossible, but with God all things are possible."

Matthew 19:26

HOLD ME TOGETHER

"He is before all things, and in him all things hold together."

Colossians 1:17

★

Lord,

Sometimes, it feels like my world is falling apart when hubby's deployed or gone for weeks-long exercises. Family plans come unraveled. Conversations, too. If something's going to break at the house, it picks this time to do so. Murphy hits again. I have no control. I'm overwhelmed, and heaviness mounts. But I'm not the one who placed the earth in orbit and causes it to rotate. You are. And I know circumstances and feelings aren't reliable, but You, oh God, are.

Life holds together in You. Help me to remember this—to take in a breath and allow truth to feed my thoughts and heart. Draw me with Your lovingkindness. Encircle me with Your assurance and faithfulness. You are trustworthy. Help me cast aside my own understanding and acknowledge You in all my ways (Proverbs 3:5). Cause me to rest in You regardless of what the day brings and to remain in You through its duration for a renewal of trust to help me take a breath and refocus.

For You, heavenly Father, go before me and there my world remains intact. Thank You, my God.

Amen.

SQUELCHING GOSSIP

"The words of a gossip are like choice morsels;
they go down to the inmost parts."

Proverbs 26:22

Lord,

You notice when I ignore the tug inside—the one that encourages me to tune out the whispers about that certain neighbor, friend, or my husband's command coworker. Instead, I sometimes lean in and listen. I hop on and ride the gossip train, spreading the stories a little further as I go. And You're privy to it all. The warning. The decision. The dangerous destination. Why do I fall prey to evil's temptation by giving my attention to these stories and the sin that twists them? What have I done? Forgive and help me, God.

Cleanse me of the filth seeping into my inmost parts. Help me flee from the temptation that attempts to worm its way into my heart—to hear and pass along gossip. May the words of my mouth and the meditations churning inside of my heart be pleasing to You, God (Psalm 19:14). Your love and grace lead me with righteousness to refuse corrupt talk, allowing only what builds up others. You counsel me with wisdom from Your Holy Spirit to spread life, not death. Praise You.

Amen.

GODLY FRIENDSHIPS

"Do not be misled: 'Bad company corrupts good character.'"

1 Corinthians 15:33

★

Lord,

You've brought many godly women into my life who I now consider lifelong, across-the-miles friends. I'm grateful for each one. Gratitude washes over me for the past, but I also wonder about what relationships await at our next post. Do good friends await us at this next stop—good and godly women? What about my husband and children—will they uncover buddies and coworkers who become part of their life story? What if bad influences lead one of us astray? The concern's real, but I set them at Your feet. Instead of worrying, I will trust in and rely upon You.

Wrap my family and me in holy wisdom as we land in this new space and make new friends. Help us discern the people You've chosen to impact our lives. Open our eyes to notice the people on whose lives we're to leave a mark, too. Uncover questionable motives or ungodliness that intends damage. Distance us from those influences. Thank You for iron-sharpening-iron friendships, the ones that will challenge, encourage, and correct us. And vice versa. In all, may You be glorified.

Amen.

WATCHING MY WORDS

"Nor should there be obscenity, foolish talk or coarse joking, which are out of place, but rather thanksgiving."

Ephesians 5:4

Lord,

The crass jokes unfold and foolish gibberish laced with obscenity, too. They make a wide swath within the military community, sucking in whoever stands in their way. They surround my husband on every side, attempt to splatter me, and eye our kids, too. At work, during deployment, and in the neighborhood, the back-alley talk awaits. And I'm scared that one of my family members or I will succumb. We need Your protection.

Erect barriers of wisdom around our hearts and mind, heavenly Father. Help us discern the filth that so easily entangles, and ingrain a desire deep within us to run far from it. Protect our ears, muffling the sounds that pry against Your righteousness. Place a lock on our lips concerning this foolish talk, and replace it with wisdom. For You are worthy of our thanksgiving. You place gratitude on our hearts and in our minds. You cause it to overflow. The praises, too. Because of You, my family and I shine like lights on a hill—beams of Your goodness for all to see. Glory to You, God.

Amen.

TAKING EVERY OPPORTUNITY

"Be very careful, then, how you live—not as unwise but as wise, making the most of every opportunity, because the days are evil."

Ephesians 5:15-16

Lord,

The ease of checking off my day-to-day list, rolling with the familiar, lulls me into spiritual deafness. I look up from my plans and realize I've missed Yours. You cross my path with others who need to hear about Your love, the security and hope of Your salvation. Need passes nearby, waiting for me to acknowledge it, yet my head remains down, hand to the plow, focused on my self-determined grind. Forgive me for the missed opportunities. Raise awareness in me.

Cause me to notice ministry opportunities, Holy Spirit. Remind me that the days are evil (Ephesians 5:16). Whether the outreach is large or small, sanctioned or not so much, help me make godly use of my time. You lead me in spreading love with a generous serving. If need knocks on my door, resides here in my home, arises at work, or lingers in the neighborhood, cause me to notice these opportunities to feed the poor and hungry, to welcome a stranger, and to visit the sick and the prisoner, for salvation resides in You.

Amen.

"Most of us want to see
God's power in our life,
but none of us want
to be weak enough
to depend on it."

Lisa Appelo

WHEN HE RETURNS

"However, each one of you also must love his wife as he loves himself, and the wife must respect her husband."

Ephesians 5:33

Lord,

My husband returns soon from deployment, and I'm grateful. Once he gets here, the readjustment period begins. I wonder whether it'll be rocky or smooth. For months, I've paid the bills, overseen the household chores, pseudo-single parented, taken care of the car, and donned the label of sole decision maker under our roof. That changes when he returns, and I'm concerned about the struggle to release control, involve him, and create good communication. Lord, help me.

Pry open my hand of control, Father, and help me remember to look to You for help. Remind me to hold things and activities loosely, keeping his preferences in mind. To involve him in parenting and household responsibilities again, refusing to run ahead without him or resent it when he steps in. You love me with great kindness and patience. Stir the same within me so that the words pouring from my mouth bring You glory and help establish good marital communication. You strengthen me to set aside self-seeking motives, and You give wisdom that builds my respect for him. Thank You, Father.

Amen.

GOODBYE, GRUMBLES

"Do everything without grumbling or arguing,"

Philippians 2:14

★

Lord,

You hear the listless grumbles filtering through military communities. They thrive among women, between couples, with neighbors, and even around kids. Healthcare, schools, husbands, commands—you name it—all are topics on the vine. I hear the complaints, and temptation lures me to join in. Sadly, I sometimes do. I trumpet all that's wrong versus what's right. But grumbling gets me nowhere. It leaves gratitude in the dust and empties me when I chatter or listen to the fruitless conversation. It remains outside of Your will. Help me put a stop to complaining.

Lead me in a life devoid of grumbling, heavenly Father. Refocus my view to see the good in people and circumstances. Remind me that these simple words are part of the battle against evil, not people. Fortify me against inklings of dissatisfaction so that I'll refuse to listen to or share them. Settle on my lips words of life, of thanksgiving, praise, kindness, and love. Because of You, my heart overflows with gratitude. Because of Your love, my words and actions emit the fragrance of Christ, spreading Your beautiful aroma. Thank You, my Deliverer. All the glory and power are Yours.

Amen.

FREEDOM FROM BITTERNESS

"Get rid of all bitterness, rage and anger, brawling and slander, along with every form of malice."

Ephesians 4:31

Lord,

Bitterness clings to me. Why can't I shake it? My husband has wronged me. His words and actions hurt me, and I'm left struggling to squash quippy, retaliatory thoughts. As the hurt festers inside of me, a wall builds between us thanks to this bitterness. My marriage suffers as a result. I fight the bite in my heart, but it takes root, leaving me in an emotional and spiritual mess. This isn't good for me or my marriage, and I want to be rid of this spiritual rancor, but I'm weak. Father, I need You.

Open wide the motivations of my heart. I've been apart from You. Forgive me for attempting to maneuver alone through this hurt. Stitch my heart's wounds with threads of Your love. Uproot this bitterness and heal me, Great Physician. Because You generously coat me with forgiveness, I choose to forgive my husband. You promise that You remain in me when I remain in You. You cause forgiveness, kindness, and gentleness to fruit (John 15:4). Your patience settles and reassures me, and I'm grateful.

Amen.

WORDS WITH ACCOUNTABILITY

"'But I tell you that everyone will have to give account on the day of judgment for every empty word they have spoken.'"

Matthew 12:36

Lord,

Words sometimes roll off of my tongue with a gentle, loving flow. Other times, they blow past my lips like a tornado bent on destruction. Later, I often feel bad for every hard-edged word spoken. If only I could unsay what I've said. Quipping harsh comebacks does good for no one. It only brings further turmoil, and I'm sorry. Forgive me, and help me keep close watch on my words.

Shake me empty of the useless vocabulary. Wipe words of death from my mind. Instead, help me communicate in a way that loves others and honors You. Imprint into my thoughts and across my lips a vocabulary carefully chosen, one emanating from righteousness and the richness of grace and mercy. Coat my thoughts with great discernment. Because of Your love, I can refuse corrupt talk. Because of You, my words build up others, because they're syllables packed with a hefty dose of grace and washed anew in righteousness. And because of You, I find forgiveness for every hasty utterance. Praise be to God.

Amen.

BUILDING UP WITH WORDS

"Better to live in a desert than
with a quarrelsome and nagging wife."

Proverbs 21:19

Lord,

I confess that a critical spirit festers in me far too often. My husband often lands in the crosshairs of my judgmental comments. I make note of how he's fallen short or missed the mark. I focus with intent on the wrong piece of the puzzle, failing to notice what's good, right, and possible. Gentleness and kindness disappear, while nagging charges forward. You know this hurts our relationship, and it disrespects him. I'm so sorry. Help me build him up, Lord, not tear him down.

Cause my heart to meditate on all that pleases You. Demolish the condemnation that chips away at love. Build my thoughts on the foundation of all that's true, noble, right, pure, lovely, admirable, excellent, and praiseworthy (Philippians 4:8). Your insight helps me formulate uplifting words that encourage my husband and shower him with respect. Your love enables me to comment and ask questions that build up my marriage. With You going before me, I communicate life, not death. I'm grateful You care and help me change. Thank You for helping me love him well with words, Lord.

Amen.

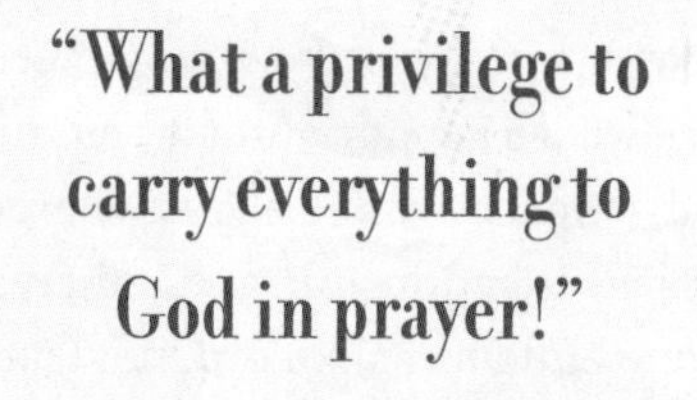

Joseph M. Scriven,
"What a Friend We Have in Jesus"

AS DEPLOYMENT APPROACHES

"Now may the Lord of peace himself give you peace at all times and in every way. The Lord be with all of you."

2 Thessalonians 3:16

Lord,

As deployment approaches, You sense the tension building between my husband and me. The uncomfortable strain ignites arguments. My reckless words cut him, giving rise to hurt feelings. He sometimes does the same. We become distant to self-protect. As I think about his departure, fear and anxiety taunt me. I don't want him to leave, but he's ordered to go. So just go already—that's how I feel. To navigate well these days leading up to deployment, I need You. Help me, Lord.

Strengthen me, almighty God, for these pre-deployment days. Forgive my careless words and actions—for taking matters into my own hands versus trusting You. Build up my faith muscles to pursue peace and live out each pre-deployment day with Your calm reassurance. Help me keep eternity in focus. Cause wisdom to churn within me—wisdom that births life-giving, marriage-edifying words. Ground me with a trust that tears down those self-made walls, for You are the God who goes before me, and Your peace surrounds me in every way.

Amen.

SAVE ME FROM SELF

"Those who trust in themselves are fools,
but those who walk in wisdom are kept safe."

Proverbs 28:26

Lord,

Sometimes, I'm my harshest critic. You watch as I measure myself against the other women. I compare my abilities, accomplishments, and body against other command wives, moms, coworkers, and women at church. And I fall short. Sometimes, I attempt something new, and if I fail, my inner critic sounds off with comments and judgment that I'd never heap on anyone else. So why do I allow these harsh thoughts to coat me? Save me from myself, Lord.

I don't want to trust myself over You. Forget defining my worth via a self-proclaimed measuring stick. Father, I long to rest in Your wisdom and ways. Forgive me for entertaining the lie that I don't measure up. Set me free from the thoughts, determinations, and self-judgment that badger and battle against my faith and Your purposes. Instead, fill me with Your wisdom. Prop me up with solid understanding to run this faith race without comparing myself to others or to perfection. Lace my decisions and thoughts with Your fulfilling grace. For You lead me with faithfulness and love. And I'm astounded, Lord.

Amen.

HELP FROM ABOVE

"I lift up my eyes to the mountains—
where does my help come from?
My help comes from the LORD,
the Maker of heaven and earth."

Psalm 121:1-2

★

Lord,

My husband's oath means I signed up for this military lifestyle, too. When he's gone, though, the weight of parenting alone crushes me. No one prepared me for this. As I scrub dishes at midnight, my shoulders sag under the weight of exhaustion. Life blurs when children cry during the dark hours. Daytime, too. No doubt You watch as I fuss and question if I can do this. But a whisper inside of me assures that if look up, I'll find help. So, Father, I look upward to You. Please meet my need.

My help comes from You, almighty God. When I'm crying out in the quiet of my home or stumbling through the day-to-day, cause me to remember this. Tilt my focus heavenward. Bathe me in Your wisdom to recognize yeses and nos that balance my family's schedule, not run me thin. Remain at the center of my need. Set on my lips the strength to seek out help when needed, or bring it my way. For You are faithful, Father.

Amen.

WHEN HE DEPLOYS

"Cast all your anxiety on him because he cares for you."

1 Peter 5:7

Lord,

Watching him leave sucks away my breath. When he walks away, decked out in the uniform of the day and with his bag slung over his shoulder, my insides tear apart. The vision sears into my memory. What if it's the last time I see him alive? What if he comes back injured or emotionally changed? Will he be okay? Will I? I feel the weight on my shoulders and anxiety building, yet You assure me this load isn't mine to carry, that I can trust You. Lord, help me hand this to You.

I run to You, Father. Reconcile the memory of his leaving with a deep trust in You. Take this anxiety. Steady me, instead, with Your love. You ground me with salvation, with hope set on the solid rock. You focus my thoughts on eternity with You, where love and peace reign. Settle the words on my lips to pray for my husband and myself and to offer You praise, for You are good. You satisfy me, calming my fears and blanketing my sadness. You coat my anxiety with Your everlasting love.

Praise You.

Amen.

DENYING TEMPTATION

"And lead us not into temptation,
but deliver us from the evil one."

Matthew 6:13

Lord,

Marriage is fragile, especially military unions. One double take or slipping in a second look and temptation swings open wide the door to lust's domain. When loneliness nags at my husband or me because we've been apart for weeks on end, we might be tempted to take that step over the threshold and break the covenant we made with each other and You. But danger lurks there—for our hearts and our marriage. I don't want this. Your Word assures me that You don't either. Deliver my husband and me from this evil.

Fortify my marriage against lust and adultery. Lay bare temptation that might come against our intimacy, communication, desire, mental health, and faith. Shield my eyes from lust's goods, whether emotional bonds or physical ones, that attempt to snare me with a "must have" cry. Protect my husband, too. You deliver him and me from evil; cause us not to fall. In our weakness, You are our strength. Reinforce the three-way tie between You, my husband, and me, Lord. For Yours is the kingdom and power forever.

Amen.

"I prayed to God to make me strong and able to fight, and that's what I've always prayed for ever since."

Harriet Tubman

HELP ME WAIT

"Those who hope in the LORD will renew their strength.
They will soar on wings like eagles; they will run
and not grow weary, they will walk and not be faint."

Isaiah 40:31

Lord,

Hurry up and wait—that's military life. You look on as I bide time concerning hubby's orders, the housing list, his return and promotion, and a million other things, including my walk with You. Too often, I tire of the wait, especially when it concerns faith. The world lulls me with justification to fill my need—now. This self-serving attitude doesn't bode well for my relationship with You. As a result, I run ahead. Busyness and disobedience flank me. Frustration overwhelms. Disappointment leads. And it's not okay. Forgive me.

Teach me to wait on You, Holy Father. Settle within me a deep trust because of Your unyielding love. When I'm tempted, remind me that You are not slow to fulfill Your promises. Weave within me patience for strength and heart for the wait. You long to be gracious to me. You rise up to show me compassion (Isaiah 30:18). You hear my voice, and that satisfies me. You enable me to wait well, and I'm grateful.

Amen.

TREASURING CONTENTEDNESS

"I have learned the secret of being content
in any and every situation, whether well fed
or hungry, whether living in plenty or in want."

Philippians 4:12b

Lord,

A house that filled our needs yesterday suddenly falls short today. A pantry of possibilities yields no good meals at first glance. The budget lands us short—again. Complaints about my husband's command, healthcare, and military lifestyle simmer then warm until unhappiness brews a large cup of discontentment. And here I am, gulping down its offering. But I don't want to live a life swirling with negativity, of complaining, and of thoughts opposed to Yours. Instead, help me find contentedness in all things.

You are my God, the one who fills my needs. You go before me, and in You all things hold together (Colossians 1:17), including my thoughts and attitude. Whether my husband's home or away, or our bank account houses extra funds or threatens to run dry, help me keep Your way in view. Bathe me in contentedness because of Your love, grace, and faithfulness. Settle in me words of life, not death. Of possibility in You.

Thank You, gracious Father.

Amen.

HOMECOMING AFTER COMBAT

"Love is patient, love is kind. It does not envy, it does not boast, it is not proud."

1 Corinthians 13:4

★

Lord,

Combat crushed our fairy-tale reunion. I sense my husband's distance in word and touch. It catapults me to fear and anger-filled thoughts. I wonder if the combat-filled visions he replays and the sounds reverberating in his ears will put a wedge between us. I want to rouse him to share, yet wisdom whispers to wait. I long to trust in You, but patience hovers in some outside corridor while faith feels far too delicate. I need You, Lord.

Muster within me God-sized love, a constant feeding that helps me navigate this unfamiliar and tough terrain. Lead me through this reintegration and beyond with patience and kindness. Cause me to see my husband through Your eyes. Open my ears that I may truly hear the underlying spiritual current of his words. I trust You. Love from above surrounds me, enabling me to protect, trust, and persevere during this time of uncertainty. Because of You, I cast aside self-seeking motives and, instead, honor You and respect my husband as he reestablishes his footing at home, work, and in our marriage.

Amen.

DOING TO OTHERS

"So in everything, do to others what you would have them do to you, for this sums up the Law and the Prophets."

Matthew 7:12

Lord,

I struggle with how to treat others at times, viewing my life as my own. I forget that You, Jesus, bought me at a price. I end up living for my needs alone. Forgive me for this self-focus and complacency. Neither of these further Your Kingdom. Help me stave off this selfishness in order to take notice of others and their needs. Show me how to love other people as I'd have them love me.

I desire to do good for the people You place in my path—to love them with an outcropping of Your love. Open my eyes to need, Lord. Cause me to notice. Hone my focus with Your wisdom, for You are the true giver of hearing and sight. You cause me to consider how to stir up others to love and good works. Your love leads me in humility so that I consider others above myself, looking to their interests over mine (Philippians 2:3-4). Thank You for pouring out Your love onto me and all the world, Jesus.

Amen.

GOOD NEIGHBORS

"Do not plot harm against your neighbor,
who lives trustfully near you."

Proverbs 3:29

Lord,

As my husband and I prepare for our upcoming move, I wonder about our new neighbors. Who will they be? Surely, You have a family in mind. Will they be outgoing or keep to themselves? Will we find lifelong friends in them? I'm curious, nervous, and unsure. I hope for open-armed, welcoming folks next door that we treasure like gold, but reality whispers of all their possible shortcomings and the difficulties we could face. Instead of siding with concern and wasting my effort, gather my thoughts into prayers.

You prepare the way, for Your good plans include hope and a future—not harm. I'm grateful, Holy Father, for this eternal promise. Lead us with Your goodness concerning our neighbors-to-be, too. You know who lives next door to the place we'll soon call home. Prepare them. Prepare us. Ready the neighborhood, too. Lead us and our new neighbors to live within the boundaries of love and trust, not harm—to think more highly of each other versus self. Your love and strength enable us to live in this manner, and I give You praise, almighty God.

Amen.

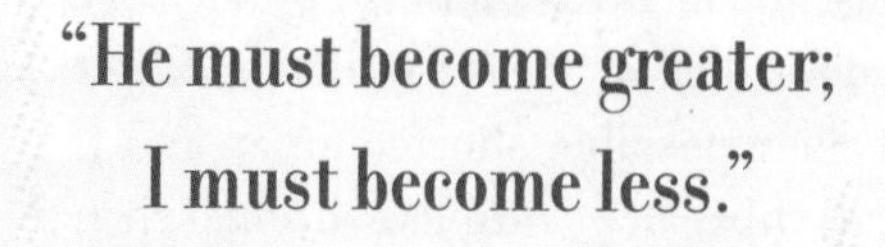

"He must become greater;
I must become less."

John 3:30

WITNESSING WHEN LIFE'S BUSY

"But you will receive power when the Holy Spirit comes on you; and you will be my witnesses in Jerusalem, and in all Judea and Samaria, and to the ends of the earth."

Acts 1:8

Lord,

You poured Your grace out on me at the cross. I now stand firm with forgiveness and salvation because of this enormous love. Thank You! I want to share this hope with others, but the busyness of life distracts me. I forget the root thrust of my faith, keeping tabs on a full schedule instead. But no more. Lives are at stake. Embolden me to share this hope I have—to be a fruitful witness for Christ.

Open my eyes. Lead me to the lost. You deliver me from fear and coat me in wisdom. May my light shine in such a way that all see. Cause my works and words to speak of Your glory—to point others to the hope they can find in You, Jesus. No shame resides in the gospel, for it is Your power for the salvation for those who believe (Romans 1:16). Praise You for conquering death, gifting life eternal, and empowering me to point others toward You.

Amen.

NEIGHBORHOOD LIGHT

"In the same way, let your light shine before others, that they may see your good deeds and glorify your Father in heaven."

Matthew 5:16

Lord,

You saved me from sin. Gratitude washes over me at the thought. Your salvation solidifies hope in my heart. The fact that You plucked me from the clutch of hell astounds and relieves me. It grounds me for these days here on earth, and I hope it witnesses to my neighbors, too. Sometimes, though, I keep things under wraps too much, like a basket placed over a light. Forgive me, Lord. Whether the days hold good or bad, help me shine Your hope for all the neighborhood to see.

Prepare me as we head to this new post. Cause neighboring nonbelievers and believers to notice Your righteous and loving ways in me. Draw their attention toward my good works—ones that I accomplish not for selfish purposes but for Your glory (Matthew 5:16). Spread Your glorious light to the people living beside us and throughout the neighboring streets. Cross my path with others, and embolden me. Your everlasting love beacons hope. Your peace guides followers on level paths. Praise be to You, God.

Amen.

STANDING FIRM

"Put on the full armor of God, so that you can take your stand against the devil's schemes."

Ephesians 6:11

Lord,

You've prepared me for spiritual battles, but lately, I'm struggling. Everywhere I turn, a fight is waiting. The kids nit-pick, things at the command turn upside down, milk spills, and miles distance me from my husband and family members. Will there be a break? Because, Lord, I'm war-weary. I confess I sometimes wonder how or if I'll withstand the daily arrows of the enemy. I don't want to fall, but my flesh objects. Help me stand strong in You and in Your mighty power.

Remind me to pick up my armor when I've set it down. Cause me to use the sword of Your powerful Word fluently. Strengthen my grip on the shield of faith to believe when healing or deliverance has yet to unfold. Balance my stance with truth latched around me, and cause righteous thoughts and decisions to protect my heart. Your gospel of peace readies my feet, and Your salvation protects my thoughts. Because of You and the armor You've fitted me with, I stand firm against the enemy's advance. This battle isn't mine, but Yours.

Amen.

FINDING PRAISE

"Why, my soul, are you downcast?
Why so disturbed within me?
Put your hope in God, for I will yet
praise him, my Savior and my God."

Psalm 42:5

Lord,

I don't love it here. It isn't what I'd hoped for—not the living quarters, local topography, weather, or my husband's work. Yet, You led us to this location, so why the downcast spirit? I want to trust and obey You—to voice gratitude and praise—but life here weighs on me like a thousand-pound block of concrete. Complaints eat at my thoughts and relationships. Negativity threatens to consume me. And fitting in? Forget it. But I know You don't delight in this attitude. Save me from this dark thinking, Lord. Help me find praise.

Wipe away the infected thoughts, Lord. Point me toward that which is good and right, all that's praiseworthy, for You are my God. Center my meditations there. You instill hope into my day and life. You lift my eyes and cause me to see relationships and plans from an eternal view. Regardless of what comes, you enable me to always hope—to praise You more and more (Psalm 71:14). Thank You for Your enduring love.

Amen.

GUARDING MY WORDS

"Those who guard their mouths and their tongues keep themselves from calamity."

Proverbs 21:23

Lord,

Sometimes, I share too much information. I hear about the comings and goings of my husband's deployments and exercises. Thanks to the command and our ombudsman, I know schedule changes, countries he'll set foot in, and the time he'll return. And sometimes, I'm tempted to share this information with family, close friends, on social media, and even private military spouse groups. But if I don't guard my words and the information I share on social media, I might put my husband and his command in danger's way. Help me be wise about what I keep close and what I choose to share. Help me guard my words.

Cause me to notice what's swirling in my thoughts about the schedules and updates I intend to share. Raise the warning flag, Holy Spirit, when I'm about to divulge too much information. Remind me to do my part to protect my husband and his coworkers. You generously pour out Your wisdom when I ask for it. You coat my words with truth and prudence. You lead me triumphantly in this as well. Thank You, almighty God.

Amen.

“He who kneels the most stands the best.”

DL Moody

SPEAKING LIFE

"Those who consider themselves religious
and yet do not keep a tight rein on their tongues
deceive themselves, and their religion is worthless."

James 1:26

Lord,

Thank You for my husband. He gifts me his love, time, and attention. It's good. When military wives gather, however, husband bashing often hijacks the conversation. A little nit-pick here, another one there—all under the guise of harmless sharing. No doubt You notice how this undercuts relationships. I keep careful watch over my words most of the time, sharing what's good and right about my husband. After marital disagreements, however, I'm tempted to vent my frustration to others. I don't want to harm him or our relationship with careless words. Help me keep a tight rein on my tongue.

Strengthen my knees when they threaten to buckle so that I can stand firm against negative chatter. Help me flee from temptation, speaking life and eating of its fruit instead of death's rotting growth. Cause my words to drip with a gracious, honey-like flow that brings sweetness and health to those who hear and to me as well. Your love leads me with kindness, not arrogance or rudeness. May my tongue do the same.

Amen.

BIDDING FAREWELL TO FRIENDS

"My comfort in my suffering is this:
Your promise preserves my life."

Psalm 119:50

Lord,

Goodbyes claw at my gut. It's hard waving farewell and driving off. When friends leave first, though, it hurts worse. I know I should find gratitude and cherish the good memories, and most of the time I do. Sometimes, though, sadness slips in and trips me up. I yearn for those deep conversations with my friend, the neighbor that made living next door to them easy, and for the local girlfriend bonds now tethered across the miles. Father, change this sad and restless outlook I house. Please comfort me.

Help me sop up these tears and keep a right frame of mind—to let gratitude lead my thoughts. You have blessed me with God-fearing girlfriends. Thank You. You're a connector of people, and I'm so thankful to be called Your daughter. Use this long-distance friendship for Your glory. Cause me to remember intentional prayer and connection, and to not let this relationship drift away. Your promises preserve my life. You give me hope, so I'll focus on things above, not below. Truly, You are my true Comforter, and I love You.

Amen.

FINDING MY MISSION

"Do not withhold good from those to whom it is due, when it is in your power to act."

Proverbs 3:27

Lord,

My family's a mission field, and I'm grateful for them. I can't help wonder, though, if outside ministry needs await us at the next stop, too. If so, what are they? With hubby's fluid schedule, church activities filling the calendar, and kids of varying ages romping around under our roof, I want to ensure I hear you clearly. Lead us to the outreach that glorifies You—one that fits us well yet stretches my family and me, too.

Here I am, Lord. Send me. I will declare Your marvelous works among the people (Psalm 96:3), whether they are sick, poor, orphaned, or widowed. Point my family and me to the people of Your eye to help meet their needs and shine the light of Christ. Show us the ministries You have in mind that glorify You. Because of Your love for us, my feet and those of my family can deliver good news to the corners of our neighborhood, the kids next door, the military installation, civilian community, and even the world. Praise You, Jesus.

Amen.

HOUSE BLESSING

"The LORD's curse is on the house of the wicked,
but he blesses the home of the righteous."

Proverbs 3:33

★

Lord,

We're settling into this new space. It's home. We'll fill it with beds, chairs, a desk, pictures, and a sofa. We'll build forever memories here. Friendships, too. We'll hold good conversations yet find ourselves challenged to overcome miscommunications, too. We don't want evil to reign in this space but love and righteousness. Our house wouldn't be a home without You. So, Lord, we invite You here. Protect and bless this house.

Fill this space. From wall-to-wall and room-to-room, let Your Spirit flow in us and all who enter. Keep evil outside these walls. You bless us, keep us, and make Your face shine upon us, and You alone give us true peace (Numbers 6:24-26). May our lives reflect it and this home be a haven for it—for all who enter, too. Cause generosity to overflow here whether through guests or those of us who reside here. Challenge us in love, joy, patience, kindness, goodness, faithfulness, gentleness, and self-control too. But most of all, may praise and thanksgiving overflow our lips, for You are worthy.

Amen.

QUIETING NEIGHBORHOOD QUIBBLES

"Like one who grabs a stray dog by the ears is
someone who rushes into a quarrel not their own."

Proverbs 26:17

Lord,

Neighborhood quibbles spark from time to time. One wife parks in another one's spot. A family dog barks endlessly. Loud music blares in and out of several doorways, and kids next door to one another go head-to-head. If I'm not careful, I'll be drawn into these arguments, too. Whether out in the open or with whispers behind the scenes, I'm lured to pick sides and jump into things. But, Lord, I don't want to turn left or right. Lead me, instead, on Your straight and narrow.

You assure me my battle isn't against flesh and blood, but it's of a spiritual nature. Focus my sight in heavenly ways, not earthly. Remind me that these quarrels are not mine, Father. Cause my feet to pause and thoughts to gather in prayer versus rushing into an argument's fire. You bless peacemakers and call them children of God (Matthew 5:9). You immerse me in wisdom for all of life's relationships, including those with other military families. Jesus, thank You for showing me the way. I will walk in it.

Amen.

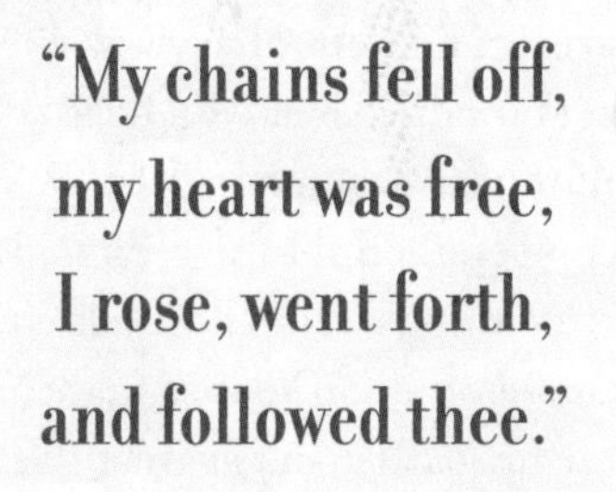

"My chains fell off,
my heart was free,
I rose, went forth,
and followed thee."

Charles Wesley,
"And Can It Be"

SET TO IMPRESS

"But if you show favoritism, you sin
and are convicted by the law as lawbreakers."

James 2:9

Lord,

I sometimes relate to people according to their stripes, achievements, and status instead of appreciating them simply as works of Your hands. Why the smoothing of my creases for those of higher rank yet not the same for others? I want to set a good impression on behalf of my husband and balance things well for his career, but aren't we all, regardless of our lot in life, people in need of You? This tug-of-war with favoritism concerns me. Help me keep my eyes off of worldly favorites and locked on You instead.

You show no partiality, calling sinners with Your love. You died for all, Jesus, and allow me to view folks through the lens of grace. Blind me to man's favorites while balancing respect for my husband. Ignite a fire in me for Your purposes, not the world's. Show me who's hungry that they might eat of eternal hope. Take me to the thirsty and use me to lead them to living water. Shine Your light in me for all to see that they might know You, Jesus.

Amen.

HARD WORKING HUSBAND

"Those who work their land will have abundant food,
but those who chase fantasies will have their fill of poverty."

Proverbs 28:19

★

Lord,

I watch my husband head off to work, and I thank You for providing his employment. You take care of him and us. He labors with diligence—sometimes full of energy, sometimes weary. I pray that he finds the strength and continues to give effort without distraction—that he refuses the everyday grind attempting to lull him into complacency or discontentedness. May he remain focused on You, not chasing empty fantasies. Help him remain energized, focused, and hard working at his job.

Your Word assures that those who work their land will have abundant food. Strengthen my husband to continue working with diligence. You've called us to do everything as if doing it unto You, including work. Fine-tune my husband's hearing concerning this, and lead him with righteousness. May he unyieldingly follow You to a deeper trust and solid obedience, surrounded by joy in the process. You cause faithful men—not those focused on wealth—to abound in blessings (Proverbs 28:20). May his faith deepen and blessings overflow onto him, for truly You are our Provider.

Amen.

GENEROUS SPIRIT

"Those who give to the poor will lack nothing,
but those who close their eyes to them receive many curses."

Proverbs 28:27

Lord,

Each month, we calculate our monthly budget down to the penny, and I struggle against a temptation to hoard what we have. I consider pulling it close and using it for ourselves, because fear spouts off about an empty wallet or bank account when need comes. But You've not called me to live a self-absorbed life, but one of generous love freely gifting my time, talents, and money for Your causes. Spring within me a generous, giving spirit.

Lord, protect me from the love of money and bowing the knee to fear. Dig up any thriving root within me that loves wealth more than You and craves cash over righteousness. Help me notice the plight of others and be drawn to action. Soften my heart toward people and their needs. Loosen my fist so that I'll live with a wide-open palm for You and others. Jesus, You generously gave Your life to cleanse me of sin and to promise eternity in heaven. Your example of selflessness continues to lead me. Praise and thanks to You.

Amen.

FINDING CALM AMID ANGER

"Fools give full vent to their rage,
but the wise bring calm in the end."

Proverbs 29:11

Lord,

Sometimes, when my husband and I converse about tough topics, my anger ignites into rage-filled flames. The fiery reaction blisters my husband's heart. Mine too. The damage this full-vent causes between us saddens me. I cringe knowing that You stand privy to these exchanges, too. I refuse to allow anger to incinerate my marriage and negatively impact other relationships. Instead, may my words and actions glorify You. Help me, Lord, process my emotions and keep anger in check.

Alert me to any sin that brews beneath my anger. Unearth the root cause behind my uncontrolled emotional responses. Forgive and heal me, almighty God. Cast off that which I'm not meant to carry. Cool my heated exchanges to a temperature and form that glorifies You, not sin or darkness. You enable me to set a guard over my mouth and remind me to keep watch so that no corrupt talk travels over my lips. Give me ears to hear and a willing spirit. Your love covers my offenses, and Your grace abounds. And with You, nothing's impossible, even healing from anger.

Amen.

LETTING GO

"'For I know the plans I have for you,'
declares the Lord, 'plans to prosper you and not
to harm you, plans to give you hope and a future.'"

Jeremiah 29:11

Lord,

As we prepare to relocate, the rearview mirror captures my attention. I focus on what's left behind, and sadness threatens to derail me. You introduced my family and me to many wonderful people at this stop. Experiences, the landscape, church, and housing, too. Thank You for each of these. However, the heaviness of letting go and moving forward without them weighs on me. I realize I need Your heavenly plans in view.

Settle my focus ahead and on Your love, Lord. Silence the fear and the sadness that threaten me. Help me find words of rejoicing, for You alone know the plans You have for me. You make plans for good–Your glorious good. You center my days on hope, an eternal future with my Father and heaven in focus. Praise You for each person and experience playing a part in this journey, those behind and ahead of me. You are for me, not against me, and I know You'll work everything together for good.

Amen.

Taste and see that
the LORD is good;
blessed is the one who
takes refuge in him.

Psalm 34:8

THANKSGIVING AMID ABSENCE

"Give thanks in all circumstances;
for this is God's will for you in Christ Jesus."

1 Thessalonians 5:18

Lord,

He missed another holiday. I feel his absence in our family when the military whisks him away and especially when Christmas or birthdays roll around. The kids yearning for their father causes his absence to weigh on me. I want him here, too. Sadness taps at my heart when I consider all he misses with these holiday celebrations. But dwelling there takes me low and steals Your praise. Instead, teach me to settle thanksgiving in my thoughts and on my lips.

I will give thanks in all circumstances, even when my husband's absence on special days is due to duty's call. Help me stand firm in gratitude and wrapped with a willingness to search for and offer it on a regular basis. Cause thanksgiving to swell within me daily. Center my thoughts on what's good and praiseworthy—even when plans unfold differently than I'd hoped. Because You, Creator of days, thread goodness into each twenty-four hours. This is the day You have made, whether my husband is home for celebrations or away. I will rejoice and be glad today (Psalm 118:24).

Amen.

EMBRACED BY PEACE

"Let the peace of Christ rule in your hearts, since as members of one body you were called to peace. And be thankful."

Colossians 3:15

Lord,

Communication with my husband has screeched to a stop, causing my inner warning siren to scream. Something's up. Is he in harm's way? Maybe the command shut down communication? But why? Is he okay? My thoughts threaten to swirl out of control. The what-ifs badger me, luring me to think of anxiety-filled outcomes. Fear plugs in its own possibilities, creating a picture of death, destruction, and dread. Yet, I know You've not called me to live this way. I seek Your help in quieting these voices and calming me.

Surround me with Your peace, Jesus. Filter Your calming reassurance—the peace that surpasses understanding—through my thoughts. Silence anxiety's concern and fear's booming voice. Because of You, my heart is not troubled. Love assures. Your invitation to cast all of my anxieties on You enables me to face life unfazed. Because of You, I dwell in safety, not fear. Thank You, loving God, for beckoning me to rest as I wait and for holy confidence to handle whatever comes my way.

Amen.

FINDING A CHURCH HOME

"Christ himself gave the apostles, the prophets, the evangelists, the pastors and teachers, to equip his people for works of service, so that the body of Christ may be built up."

Ephesians 4:11-12

Lord,

Because of You, my family and I found a strong support network, small group, Sunday services, prayer warriors, children's service, and musical worship with our last set of orders. Each person exercised unique spiritual strengths that fed into my life and my family members' lives. You allowed us to pour into others, too. Thank You for leading us to a solid church home. Life and another relocation call us to do it again. Lord, lead us to our new church home.

Root my family and me in a congregation that worships You in spirit and in truth. Guide us to a faith-filled, Bible-teaching pastor and worship family, a church where salvation and love run rich—spiritual fruit and service, too. Use my family members and me to build others up in faith, and surround us with those who'll aid in our spiritual maturity. Holy Spirit, You endow us with wisdom and discernment as we search for our next spiritual home. I give You thanks.

Amen.

FAVOR WITH HIS BOSS

"Now God had caused the official to show favor and compassion to Daniel,"

Daniel 1:9

★

Lord,

Thank You for my husband's chain of command, especially for his immediate and close supervisors. A boss can make or break contentment–advancement and career, too, and You watch as they go about their business. These men and women fill important roles, and their decisions affect my husband, our family, and others. But You are still God of gods and anything is possible with You, so I bring my petition to You concerning my husband. Please help him find favor with his boss.

Lord, You reign above all, causing the hearts of men to turn. Soften the hearts of those in authority over my husband, especially his immediate supervisor. If he (or she) doesn't know You, draw them in a way that they'll be captured for eternity. Turn heated situations into ones that glorify You, and like Daniel, protect my husband. Wherever he steps his foot, may Your favor go before him. But not for his glory–for Yours, heavenly Father. May the world see, or at least those nearby, and shout Your praises. For You are my husband's Provider, Defender, and Healer.

Amen.

APPROACHING RETIREMENT

"Surely God is my help;
the Lord is the one who sustains me."

Psalm 54:4

Lord,

My husband's military retirement faces us. We've looked forward to this day for years, yearning for it at times. But my stomach knots concerning this new chapter in life now standing in front of us. Where should we live? What about the three-year moving bug? Will we find jobs, meet the budget, and land in a solid church? What if the adjustment proves rocky? Will we be okay? Lord, only You know. Reassure and prepare my family and me.

You number the hairs on my head and note that I'm worth more than the sparrows (Luke 12:7). You are my faithful Provider. I'll not be afraid. Guide me with wisdom as we step into the civilian world. Crush the anxiety when it wells within me. Remind me that You know my needs and those of my family. You shepherd me, and I have no want. The Scriptures train me in righteousness; they equip my family and me for every good work in this next chapter (2 Timothy 3:16-17). Thank You, Lord, that my family and I will be okay because of You.

Amen.

"Prayer is a long rope with a strong hold."

Harriet Beecher Stowe

RAISING GODLY KIDS

"Do not worry about tomorrow, for tomorrow will worry about itself. Each day has enough trouble of its own."

Matthew 6:34

Lord,

Gratitude fills me concerning my kids. They're Your handiwork, but apprehension needles at me. Will they grow up and be okay? I worry about their dad's frequent absences and schedule instability. They need him. Unease squeezes my heart when I think about the rotation of schools and churches they'll experience before adulthood, the numerous goodbyes and differing cultures they'll be expected to adapt to, and the absence of extended family. I need Your peace, Lord, regarding my children. Please protect them.

Wipe away my worries about my kids' future, for they were bought with a price. You reassure me that Your love for my children runs deeper than my own. May their admiration, worship, and love for You deepen by the day. You know every hair on their head. May their identity rest in You alone. Thank You for equipping their father and me to train them in the way they should go. May they go in it and not depart from You (Proverbs 22:6). And Lord, thank You for Your love which banishes all fear.

Amen.

MY WORK

"She sets about her work vigorously;
her arms are strong for her tasks."

Proverbs 31:17

Lord,

We set off with our next orders soon, and I wonder what—or if—employment waits for me. You know our needs, but will doors open? Transient military spouses often fall short on the hire list, and I wonder if this job-hunting effort will follow suit. Worry nips at me, but Your faithfulness reassures me. So today, I run to Your throne and bring this need. Father, prepare my heart for the job search and an offer. Open wide the doors that are Yours.

Through it all, You've always been with me. Thank You. I commit this search and the subsequent work to You. Lead me to employment that brings You glory, a position in which I can work heartily for You. Brush away anything that clouds my view of the path before me. Prepare the workplace so that even there I glorify You. Ready me and my future employer, too. Flood me with Your wisdom, Holy Spirit, to search through a righteous lens and to accept or decline accordingly. You give me hope and strength for life, a thrust to work vigorously.

Amen.

CREATING A HOME

"By wisdom a house is built, and through understanding it is established; through knowledge its rooms are filled with rare and beautiful treasures."

Proverbs 24:3-4

★

Lord,

Orders take us from place to place with new living quarters at each stop. The structures assigned to us appear different each time, remaining mysterious and undesignated until we arrive. I itch to know what our new address offers. You see the dwelling. You know. Is it small? Maybe large? Do sparse and cold etch their typical military mark on the rooms? Regardless, space makes no matter. Four walls don't make a home. Love does. Infuse Your everlasting love into these new living quarters.

Help us create a true home, a space and atmosphere roughed out and finished with love. Fill our conversations with grace and our kitchen with food that satisfies both the stomach and the heart. Let wisdom filter our thoughts and actions. Aid me to place furnishings in ways that encourage godly conversations, inside and outside. May gentleness flow through the hallways and peace in the bedrooms, reassuring occupants and visitors, too. Your knowledge establishes our home, creating a peaceful, secure space. Here, we serve You and give You praise.

Amen.

COMMUNICATING WELL

"A gentle answer turns away wrath,
but a harsh word stirs up anger."

Proverbs 15:1

Lord,

My husband and I sometimes struggle with communication. When hurt pings at my heart, I hide behind a self-constructed wall, and conversation refuses to flow. Other times, my words cut through our conversation like a sharp knife slicing paper. In some instances, he reacts similarly. These reactions hurt both of us. Harsh words only pierce hearts. Silence does similarly. So why do I allow them? Help me, Lord, communicate in a godly manner.

Render within me a heart's desire for listening and lending an ear quickly—to You and my husband. Instill godly hearing in both my heart and ears, heavenly Father, that You might be glorified by my husband's and my communication. Take my self-will and send it outside. Banish self-protection, too. Settle patience and wisdom on my vocal chords and lips, a willingness to measure my responses and requests against Your righteousness. Your strength and wisdom cause me to consider and utter meaningful words, ones that ignite godly conversation and serve loving solutions, not anger or self-righteousness. Because of You, the words of my mouth and meditations of my heart are pleasing.

Amen.

PREPARE ME

"Let your conversation be always full of grace, seasoned with salt, so that you may know how to answer everyone."

Colossians 4:6

Lord,

Prepare me to share of Your goodness. So many in this military community house an emptiness filled only by You. For salvation and for day-to-day needs too. Only You offer true hope, and I want to share this with the world—with everyone I come in contact with this week in hopes they'll take up Your offer of eternity in heaven. Somehow, though, I either stumble over my words or they get caught deep in my throat and lose purpose. When people ask questions or challenge my faith, I flounder. Help me formulate answers, Lord. Prepare me.

Deliver me from fear, pride, and the enemy's tactics to confuse my thoughts and words, for my true help comes from above. It comes from You, Maker of heaven and earth. Fill my conversation with an overflow of grace. Season my words, Holy Spirit, with a noticeable flavor of wisdom that causes others to take notice, a tongue of wisdom that commends knowledge (Proverbs 15:2). You, heavenly Father, will place the answers on my tongue, and I rest in this.

Amen.

“As you pray and believe,
God is powerfully
at work breathing
life into dark spaces.”

Lyli Dunbar

INTIMACY BETWEEN US

"The husband should fulfill his marital duty to his wife, and likewise the wife to her husband."

1 Corinthians 7:3

★

Lord,

Thank You for bringing my husband home safely. After this last deployment, though, he remains distant and pulls back from touch. Something plagues our marital intimacy, and it concerns me. Maybe conflict experiences pushed him to this place? Or something else? Whatever the cause, our happy reunion suffers as we stumble and attempt to regain our footing. Lord, I need You. Show me how to love my husband. Protect our intimacy.

Fill me with wisdom and understanding. Show me how to be his wife when intimacy suffers. Whisk me away to a place of patience, kindness, and understanding. Cause me to be gentle and self-controlled, to love him the way I want to be loved, and to love You still more. You give peace in this war. Break down and cast out that which attempts to hijack our intimate words and actions. Protect our marriage from adultery and apathy. Heal him. Heal me. Strengthen us to reserve ourselves for each other, and restore what the locust has eaten. I put my trust in You, glorious God.

Amen.

BARING MY HEART

"As water reflects the face,
so one's life reflects the heart."

Proverbs 27:19

Lord,

I live day-to-day, assured I cart around a good heart. Reactions crop up from time to time, however, that assure me something's amiss. I realize my heart needs help. I long to be humble in all circumstances, mimicking You, Jesus—walking with kindness, forgiveness, and wisdom for navigating relationships and situations with grace and mercy. But I struggle. Others may or may not see it, but You and I notice. It's time for a heart check-up. Show me what's in my heart. Lay bare anything that wars against righteousness.

You alone know me, God almighty, and this warms me. You created my every part, knitting the threads of my heart together in my mother's womb. You search my heart—the thoughts and the intentions I entertain. Fill me with discernment to identify the lies which war against Your holiness. They must go, for my body is Your house. Forgive me for siding with pride and fear. Your grace pours over and refreshes me, freeing me. Love and truth from above cloak me and lead me in the way everlasting, and You deserve my praise, Jesus.

Amen.

LISTENING WELL

"My dear brothers and sisters, take note of this:
Everyone should be quick to listen, slow to speak
and slow to become angry, because human anger does
not produce the righteousness that God desires."

James 1:19-20

Lord,

Most of the time I communicate well. During tough or emotional conversations, however, I often interrupt others. I refuse to listen, spouting off quippy or harsh responses that build, word by word, an invisible barrier between the listener and me. At that moment, I've chosen not to listen well with these ears You've given me, and I'm sorry. Forgive me. I don't want things to play out this way. Help me listen well to my husband, family, friends, and even strangers.

Remove from me the folly and shame that answer before hearing (Proverbs 18:13). Open my understanding and help me identify these less-than-best, knee-jerk responses. Pour into my heart Your wisdom and patience. I'm willing. You enable me to speak slowly and listen with a quick ear. Your love causes me to think more highly of others than myself. You coat my words with the honey of gentleness and kindness, and Your righteousness leads me in victory for today and eternity. Hallelujah!

Amen.

DISCUSSING TOUGH TOPICS

"Those who know your name trust in you, for you, LORD, have never forsaken those who seek you."

Psalm 9:10

★

Lord,

My husband I must converse about death, injury, tight finances, guardianship, burial wishes, and more. I dread it, but wisdom calls us to place our matters in order before deployment. In preparation—just in case. The *what-if* thoughts cause me to recoil, Lord. I'd rather ignore these hard-to-swallow possibilities. But that negates a solution. I need Your strength and wisdom to face these tough topics. Help me trust in You as my man and I converse and make decisions concerning life's heavy potentials.

Remind me to take captive my thoughts and place my hope in Jesus. You are my strong tower, so I run to Your trustworthy protection. Regardless of what I face and through these tough conversations, Your love reassures me. It strengthens and leads me. You, Lord, have not forsaken me—not in the past, now, or in the future. On the foundation of Your love, Jesus, I stand firm. You bathe me in wisdom because of Your generosity. My husband, too. Be glorified, Lord, as we stand with hope and make wise decisions.

Amen.

MY HUSBAND'S SALVATION

"Jesus replied, 'Very truly I tell you, no one can see the kingdom of God unless they are born again.'"

John 3:3

Lord,

Eternity lasts forever. You bridged my sin need, and my eternity now awaits in heaven. My husband, however, still eyes Your invitation without acceptance. Uneasiness drenches me when I consider my husband missing heaven. He's a good man, but hell devours men like him—respectable husbands, fathers, and community citizens. You love him dearly, and You know I do, too. Soften his heart. Make known his need for reconciliation due to sin. I pray he accepts You as his Savior, Jesus, and grace secures his salvation.

Giver of love, You assure that if my husband simply believes, he will gain eternal life. Stir within my husband a hard-core belief. The enemy yanks at his heart, though, and attempts to muffle the voice of truth. Let no weapon formed against him prosper. You cause ears to hear and hearts to awaken. Praise God! You soften hearts and prepare people for truth. Hallelujah! Open wide my husband's ears and heart to hear You calling. May he understand his need and answer with, "Yes, Lord," and be born again.

Amen.

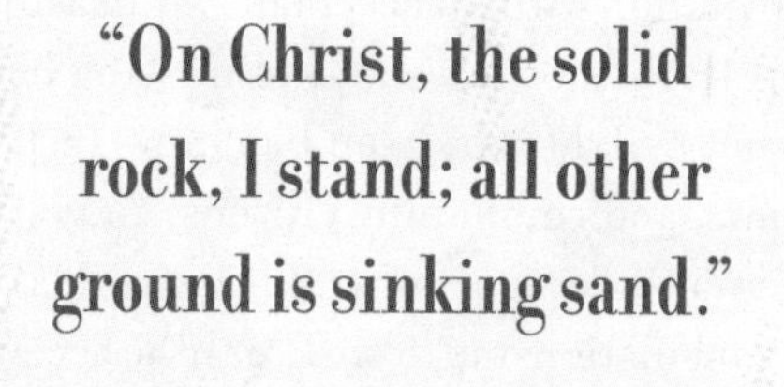

Edward Mote,
"My Hope is Built"

GOD, YOU COMPLETE ME

"Let us run with perseverance the race marked out for us, fixing our eyes on Jesus, the pioneer and perfecter of faith."

Hebrews 12:1b-2a

★

Lord,

My heart beats with gratitude for this life with my husband. I'm proof that a military wife's journey can be good and godly. So why, from time to time, do I look to my husband, not You, to complete me? No man defines and hems together another person where it matters most—in the heart. Forgive me for running first to my husband, not You. Forgive me for leaning on him and his rank or my status as a military spouse to capture fulfillment. Build my faith, God, to look fully to You for wholeness.

You created me, not man or his devices. You author and perfect my life, bridging my need with undeserving forgiveness. You mark the race for me and sanctify me completely. Strengthen me to run with fervency for Christ and Christ alone. Remind me that I am made whole and complete in You. Surely, You can do all things. Praise You, almighty One, for fixing my eyes on You and the purposes of Your glorious and eternal plan.

Amen.

REMAINING FAITHFUL

"Marriage should be honored by all,
and the marriage bed kept pure, for God will
judge the adulterer and all the sexually immoral."

Hebrews 13:4

Lord,

The promise my husband and I made before You stands—a covenant with You and each other. We entered marriage honoring one other. Love, honesty, and faithfulness fuel our relationship. As our marriage grows, I want to remain faithful and hope he does as well. Temptation, however, would like nothing more than to tear us apart. Marriages, even strong ones, are especially vulnerable during times apart. Lord, help us protect our marriage. Strengthen both my husband and me to remain faithful emotionally, spiritually, and physically.

You created man and woman, and our marriage union remains in You, Father. Help us honor our vows by keeping our marriage bed pure. Protect us from stray thoughts, dangerous emotional attachments, and physical intimacy outside of our union. Shield us with Your protection from adultery and divorce. You fill us with wisdom for making choices about where we look, who we entertain, and what we desire. May we heed wisdom's call. You reinforce our cord of three. Praise You, almighty God and keeper of Your loving covenant.

Amen.

LEARNING THE LINGO

"But the Advocate, the Holy Spirit, whom the Father will send in my name, will teach you all things and will remind you of everything I have said to you."

John 14:26

★

Lord,

This new military lifestyle comes with its own lingo, a foreign language of sorts. A sense of being overwhelmed hovers nearby as I attempt to keep straight PCS from BX, PX, and XO. I want to do our marriage justice and relate to my husband, but I can't do it if communication is cut short. If I want to enter this new military lifestyle successfully, the lingo must become a part of my vocabulary. Lord, help me decipher and remember the acronyms and abbreviations. Help me honor my husband, strengthen my marriage, and adjust to this foreign aspect of life.

Military language falls far short of spiritual things, but I believe You care about the little things in life, too. You assure me that You hear my prayers and that I should pray continually—that I have not because I ask not (James 4:2). So, I send this request heavenward. Help me find my footing with military abbreviations, forms, and terms. I trust You. Be glorified, Father, even in this.

Amen.

STAYING POSITIVE

"Rejoice in the Lord always. I will say it again: Rejoice!"

Philippians 4:4

Lord,

I love living life as a military spouse. You've blessed me with this community, making friends that we adopt like family. My days overflow with reasons for gratitude and opportunities to shower You with praise. Sometimes, though, I feel a nudge to hang my thoughts judgmentally and to focus on what's wrong. Lord, wipe away the negativity. Help me walk through this military life with a positive attitude, focusing on the good and righteous.

Your mighty deeds and goodness deserve my praise. With my breath, I will offer that praise. Many in the military hold onto negative thoughts and speak critically, finding the wrong, but You birthed a different spirit in me. When such spirits chime, remind me not to answer the call. Set out the welcome mat for thoughts that ring right and true, for praiseworthy and good words. Strengthen me to rejoice always, to pray without ceasing, and to thank You continually, for You are my rock, my fortress, and my deliverer. Because of You, I am not conformed by the world but am transformed by the renewing of my mind.

Amen.

KEEPING FAITH STRONG

"So do not throw away your confidence;
it will be richly rewarded."

Hebrews 10:35

Lord,

Your love fuels me. Your grace and mercy, too, and my gratitude grows. I long to run the race well, but lately, my faith feels cold. I read the words of my Bible, but it morphs into checks on a task list instead of an intimate encounter with You. I utter prayers, but the silence amplifies, and I struggle. My desire that once burned hot now chills. Lord, free me from this. Rescue me from this dangerous pit. Help me keep my faith strong.

As I yearn for regular communion with You in prayer and beautiful immersion in Your Word, You hear the wants of my heart. You've given me an unchanging love that pours hope into me even when life feels stale. Praise You! Whisper in my ear those assurances of things hoped for even though not yet seen. Bolster my confidence. Remind me to focus on eternal things, Lord, and on Your goodness, for You are the lifter of my head. You sharpen my spiritual eyesight and cause me to stand firm in faith. You are my God forever, and I love You.

Amen.

I urge, then, first of all, that petitions, prayers, intercession and thanksgiving be made for all people.

1 Timothy 2:1

LEAVING BITTERNESS BEHIND

"See to it that no one falls short of the grace of God and that no bitter root grows up to cause trouble and defile many."

Hebrews 12:15

Lord,

This lifestyle sounded exciting and new at first. I jumped in, ready for the adventure, but the fun wore off when my hubby deployed, schedules changed, and life turned erratic. I feel alone, and as I consider all that I left behind—life's familiarity and beloved family members—bitterness seeps in. I miss what I had. Your Word, though, rings inside of my thoughts, warning me of resentment's ploy to rob me of peace and praise. Forget embitterment. I desire to glorify You. Lord, please free me from this tug-of-war.

You search and know my heart. It lays bare before You, even the bitterness—and still, You love me. Relief coats me, gracious Father. Forgive me for allowing space for these thoughts. Help me unearth their roots and sweep away justification. Cleanse my thoughts, for You create in me a clean heart, O God. You renew a right spirit within me (Psalm 51:10). You thwart the enemy's plans and shower me in love and peace. Praise You.

Amen.

PROTECTION FROM DIVORCE

"But we prayed to our God and posted
a guard day and night to meet this threat."

Nehemiah 4:9

Lord,

My husband and I married with forever as our intent. But as I look around, I notice divorce perched on nearly every corner, ready to pounce and devour unsuspecting unions. It concerns me. Will my marriage withstand the devices of darkness? Will my husband and I draw closer to You and one another in this military journey or pull further apart as time lapses? My marriage needs You. Be my strength; protect my marriage from the grip of divorce.

Draw my husband and I closer, Lord. Grow our relationship with You and each other. Pull us in like a mother brings close her chicks. Deepen our bond as we stand firm against this threat. Reinforce our commitment to one another with a mighty dose of wisdom, Holy Spirit, and with solid communication. Tighten any loose threads with Your grace and forgiveness. You help us grow love, joy, peace, patience, kindness, goodness, faithfulness, gentleness, and self-control, knitting us together even more so. Your strength enables us to stand as we do the work to keep our marriage secure. Thank You, Father.

Amen.

BIRTH WITHOUT HIM

"Truly he is my rock and my salvation;
he is my fortress, I will never be shaken."

Psalm 62:2

Lord,

My husband's absence during this pregnancy and birth of our child saddens me. Concern grows, and anxiety creeps into my thoughts. Am I strong enough to handle this alone? Who will come alongside us? Will the pregnancy and delivery flow smoothly? What about my husband—how will he handle missing this special season of our lives? So many decisions and thoughts surround this. I fear attempting this alone. Lord, I need Your great wisdom and peace for the journey ahead.

Strengthen these feeble knees, for You are my rock and my salvation. You anchor me. I ask for Your wise counsel to guide my decisions for birthing options, medical help, trips to the hospital, assistance at home, my and the baby's health, and my husband's peace during this time. Surround us with godly, supportive friends—people who understand the needs at hand. Folks I can bless in return. Cradle our baby in Your protection both inside and outside of the womb, for this one is a heritage from You. May this child live to praise Your name.

Amen.

LETTING GO

"Set your minds on things above, not on earthly things."

Colossians 3:2

Lord,

No doubt, faithfulness runs rich in Your kingdom. I know I should trust You in all areas of my life, but sometimes, I grip self-trust with fingers clenched. You wait patiently, watching as I wrestle with anxiety and then wrestle some more. This need to control chews at me to keep dibs on things, pressing them hard under my thumb. And when life comes unwrapped, a part of me comes undone, too. Far too often. But You didn't create man to carry the load. Show me, instead, how to release this need to be in charge. Teach me how to trust You instead.

In You all things hold together. Echo this truth in my thoughts and to the depth of my heart, Lord. I want to believe and trust in You fully—with all of my heart. I cast my cares on You, Holy One. You run to my aid, dismantling anxious thoughts with a reassuring trust. For Your yoke is easy, and Your burden is light. You deliver me from this spirit of control and fill me with trust and peace. Thank You, Jesus.

Amen.

STAVING OFF COMPLACENCY

"Finally, be strong in the Lord and in his mighty power."

Ephesians 6:10

★

Lord,

My husband's job causes him to spend so much time away from me, and it wears on our relationship. Concern envelopes me. Military wives call it normal. But will "normal" birth a complacency and self-sufficiency that slides our marriage into the trouble zone? When I consider how the time apart piles up and the many birthdays, anniversaries, and holidays we endure while distanced, I grow concerned. Without You, our marriage will land in shambles. Lord, help me do my part to keep our marriage strong.

Cause my thoughts and actions to intertwine with a whole-hearted trust and dogged obedience. Reinforce me as a woman who lives under Your holy umbrella where my marriage is concerned. My husband, likewise. Settle creative ideas in our thoughts to bolster our relationship even though distance spans between us. Help us stave off complacency and temptation. Plant an eager and willing spirit within each of us to continue building a thriving marriage, not individual lives. Carry our union on the wings of Your love throughout our military tenure and beyond. For no one or nothing can stand against You.

Amen.

"Put on the gospel armor, each piece put on with prayer; where duty calls or danger, be never wanting there."

George Duffield, Jr.

"Stand Up, Stand Up for Jesus"

PROTECTION FROM COMBAT TRAUMA

"You provide a broad path for my feet,
so that my ankles do not give way."

Psalm 18:36

Lord,

My husband's combat experiences remain hidden from me, but You see him. It tears at me, thinking of the mental and physical war trauma he faces or may face. I'm a mess inside. How will he process things both during his time overseas and when he comes home? Fear grips me daily, clouding my thoughts when I consider the possibilities. I fight it off, but my strength proves to be no match. Help me pray for my husband, God, and for his protection from trauma.

Defend his body, mind, and sleep with Your shield of victory. Sustain him with Your right hand for both rough and smooth days (Psalms 18:35). Protect him against injury, and strengthen him for the journey. Coat him with love, peace, and a sound mind, settling anxiety's fierce repute. Prepare him for a successful homecoming, opening wide his communication and my understanding. Your love casts out all fear—for my husband and me. Praise You, Jesus, for showering him with courage to process experiences and find healing from combat's destruction. May the glory be Yours.

Amen.

STEPPING OUT ALONE

"For the Spirit God gave us does not make us timid, but gives us power, love and self-discipline."

2 Timothy 1:7

★

Lord,

When my husband's deployed, will I have what it takes to step out alone? To ask questions and make decisions that affect our family, him, and me? To carry on, enjoy an evening out with friends, and hold it together? I hope for a *yes,* Lord, but I know I need Your strength and guidance. Help me squash the timidity and all that attempts to restrain me from stepping out alone.

I desire to live day-to-day with an extra dose of courage. Instill in me a strong serving of boldness, one that'll lead me to ask questions when I'd rather remain quiet, to press matters versus letting them fall through, and to continue stepping in faith when evidence is lacking. Your Spirit builds me with the ability to love when difficulty stands in the way and to remain self-disciplined when I'd rather sit down, walk away, or give up altogether. Because You gave me a spirit of power, love, and self-control, I keep fear at bay. Thank You for being with me wherever I go.

Amen.

REMAINING UNDER ONE ROOF

"But Ruth replied, 'Don't urge me to leave you or to turn back from you. Where you go I will go, and where you stay I will stay. Your people will be my people and your God my God.'"

Ruth 1:16

Lord,

Military needs pull active duty members from home, including deployment, exercises, and the geo-bachelor life. I watch as families around us spend time apart then come unraveled, helped along by this distance between them. My husband and I desire to protect our relationship from this disintegration. Show us how to strengthen our marriage for those inevitable times apart. More so, help us remain under one roof as much as possible.

Fill us with Your wisdom, Holy Spirit, so that we know when to go and when to stay. Open opportunities for us to remain together as much as possible. And for those times when we're apart, lead us not into temptation. Deliver us from the evil that attempts to chip away at or completely dismantle our marriage. Because of You, God, we can keep the marriage bed pure. Because of You, we know we can ask, and You hear us. Wherever You lead us, Lord, we will follow.

Amen.

MAKING ENDS MEET

"Seek first his kingdom and his righteousness, and all these things will be given to you as well."

Matthew 6:33

Lord,

The paycheck continues to arrive, two each month. Thank You for Your provision. We live on it, even as checking account funds dip low before the next payday. I'm grateful the inflow continues and for the wisdom You've given concerning money. Worry pecks at me, though, because of our changing needs. How will our finances stretch? Or will they? I shouldn't worry, but it's hard not to when staring at numbers written in black and white. Lord, please help us make ends meet.

Forgive me for worrying. You are my provider and give as I need. You've not forsaken my family or me. Lord, I lay down the worry and pick up prayer. I set my focus on Your kingdom and righteousness, for You know the plans You have for my husband, me, and our family. You give what we truly need, whether it comes in miraculous or everyday ways. You give us our daily bread—and will with this need, too. My eyes are fixed above, for Yours, Father, is the kingdom, the power, and the glory.

Amen.

BLENDING FAMILIES WITH PEACE

"Blessed are the peacemakers,
for they will be called children of God."

Matthew 5:9

★

Lord,

Thank You for our blended family. You knit together each one of the beautiful faces, hearts, and bodies we now call "us," and Your work deserves abundant praise. As my husband and I endeavor to bond two families into one, we need You. Apart from You, my husband and I can do nothing, especially bring this family together successfully. To be a good and God-honoring stepmother, I need You. Help me bond with the children and create a peaceful atmosphere in our home.

You are the Prince of Peace. Wash us with that peace, Jesus, both eternally and moment by moment. May I be a peace--maker in this home and in the kids' lives. Understanding leads me as I step into the parenting roll. Your victory gives me hope for eternity and these relationships, too. You cause me to communicate with wisdom and patience. You strengthen me to love the children as I would myself. And You can soften our hearts to live and move and have our being in You. Prepare all of us to live in unity with each other and bring You glory.

Amen.

"If I had a choice,
I would still choose
to remain blind...
for when I die,
the first face I will ever
see will be the face
of my blessed Saviour."

Fanny Crosby

NOT WHAT I EXPECTED

"And we know that in all things God works for the good of those who love him, who have been called according to his purpose."

Romans 8:28

Lord,

Someone turned my cup of expectations upside down, spilling out the nice, tidy picture of the life I carried. It's now strewn across the floor in puddle fashion. What now? This isn't what I expected. But then again, this is military life. And detours don't surprise You, because You're an all-knowing God. Even though things aren't going the way I had hoped, I know my trust should remain in You, and I want it to. Help me corral my thoughts and rely on and trust in You.

Settle my thoughts on your overflowing provision and constant presence, loving Father. Remind me to cast my burdens versus stand with disillusionment, for You are a mighty God. You go before and don't forsake me. You assure me to refuse fear's call and to not be dismayed (Deuteronomy 31:8). I trust in You. No doubt You'll see me through this life detour and any others that may follow, as You keep in perfect peace those whose minds are stayed on You (Isaiah 26:3).

Amen.

OVERCOMING WORK DISAPPOINTMENTS

"Return to your fortress, you prisoners of hope;
even now I announce that I will restore twice as much to you."

Zechariah 9:12

Lord,

I watch my husband drag his feet across the front door threshold. His shoulders sag, and his smile fades. The weight of his demeanor nearly crushes us both. The disappointment on his face tells of another career blow. No career advancement for yet another go-round. I want to lift the load, cast it aside, and bring him instant joy. But my feeble strength doesn't compare to Yours, so I run to You. Help him recover from the disappointment. Lift his spirits where work is concerned.

We make plans, but You, oh God, establish our steps (Proverbs 16:9). Gratitude washes over me as my prayers rise to You. You establish my husband's steps concerning his advancement and career. You are the lifter of his head. Keep his focus above, for You are his God, and You lead and lavish Him with an everlasting love. Remind him to cast his anxieties at Your feet. Me too, for You, Jesus, have overcome the world. You go before my husband and never leave him. Praise You, faithful and mighty God.

Amen.

WHEN WE BOTH SERVE

"Be strong and courageous. Do not be afraid or terrified because of them, for the Lord your God goes with you; he will never leave you nor forsake you."

Deuteronomy 31:6

Lord,

It comforts me that You see my husband and me as we both serve in the military. You know our inner workings and our day-to-day. Sometimes, though, dual service is hard. It clashes with married life. He gets busy with work. Me too. Deployments steal our time together. We wrestle to find time alone and obtaining orders for spouse co-locations. Without vigilance, we'll allow the military to mold our relationship. But that's no good. Help us build our marriage on Your terms instead.

Your Word commands us to be strong and courageous. Cause those traits to fuel our marriage, too. May my husband and I be strong in You and in Your mighty power. Point us toward righteous decisions for our marriage and family as well as for us as individuals. Open doors that no other can, God, for I know that Your faith and love lead us with strength. You set a shield around us and our marriage. We've nothing to fear. Praise You, God!

Amen.

ADJUSTING TO MILITARY LIFE

"They were all trying to frighten us, thinking, 'Their hands will get too weak for the work, and it will not be completed.' But I prayed, 'Now strengthen my hands.'"

Nehemiah 6:9

Lord,

Military life's new and intimidating. Will I ever adjust, especially with my husband shipped out? Things are simple yet complex. Fluid and unfamiliar. The thought of living this lifestyle thrills me, but I also fight loneliness and fear with all the new acronyms, terms, and other notable differences. Will I ever scale this mountain in front of me, God? With You, I'm convinced I can adjust to military living, but it looks overwhelming right now. Help me find my footing.

I will not walk away from my husband or this lifestyle. The enemy slings doubt across my thoughts to make me question adjustment, but I demolish the arguments that set themselves up against the knowledge of God. You've empowered me to take captive those thoughts and make them obedient, Christ. Give me a teachable spirit and an extra dose of courage and wisdom for this time. I trust in Your unfailing love and rejoice in Your salvation, Lord (Psalm 13:5). Praise to You, oh God.

Amen.

CARING FOR MY PARENT

"Honor your father and your mother,
so that you may live long in the
land the LORD your God is giving you."

Exodus 20:12

Lord,

Thank You for the blessing of parents. I love and appreciate mine. You've called me to honor them that all might go well, and my heart beats to do so. Concerning their health and lot in life, they need me. As You see, it's not easy to care for a parent while living a military lifestyle. Worry peaks, and difficulties with care and living quarters rise, too. Help me honor Mom and Dad the way You've called me to.

Pour into me wisdom for the journey, Holy Spirit. Guide my steps with the lamp of Your Word and righteousness, for apart from You, I can do nothing that makes a difference for Your kingdom. Strengthen me to honor my parents whether they're healthy or sick, living independently or in need. Let wisdom lead me to respect and love my husband well as I honor them, too. Heavenly Father, show me how to love and take care of my parents and how to balance their needs with those of my family and my own during our days in the military.

Amen.

"When we call on Jesus,
He turns our desperate
places into doorways
to His presence."

Betsy de Cruz

DIMINISH THE DISTRACTIONS

"Let your eyes look straight ahead;
fix your gaze directly before you."

Proverbs 4:25

Lord,

Daily life and busyness pull at me. My husband deserves my time and attention—kids and far away family members as well. Friends come calling, activities clutter the calendar, and online and media chatter distracts. If I'm not careful, I'll allow life to divert my attention from You, a situation in which danger, no doubt, lies in wait. I desire to put You before all things, even that which seems good. Help me to prioritize prayer, worship, and spending time in the Word with You.

Father, fix my focus on You. Carve out a daily space where I'm free from these distractions. Set a desire so deep within me that I'll refuse to allow anything to detour my time with You. Cause me to seek You and Your kingdom first, shifting away that which averts my attention from Your righteousness. Gather my attention toward Your wisdom; incline my ear toward understanding (Proverbs 5:1). You wrap me in perfect peace because my mind is stayed on You (Isaiah 26:3). You are my dwelling place, Most High, and in Your shadow I'm relieved to abide.

Amen.

EQUIPPED FOR MENTORSHIP

"Walk with the wise and become wise,
for a companion of fools suffers harm."

Proverbs 13:20

★

Lord,

You've planted wise women in my life as mentors, and I'm ever grateful. Your goodness grows in me as a result. I've been challenged, encouraged, corrected, and built by the words and actions of these women—all in the name of Jesus. At this next stop, will I be that woman for someone else? A stirring inside of me causes me to think so, but I desire to walk in obedience and to follow Your call. Lead me as a woman of God and as a mentor, too.

Tunnel a route deep into my heart and pour in Your wisdom, Holy Spirit, that it might bubble up and overflow for discipleship. Cross my path with a woman eyeing the abundant life. Prepare her. Prepare me. Father, Your ways and paths delight me—no doubt concerning mentorship, too. Your guidance lands me in a place of hope, for You are God my Savior (Psalm 25:4-5). May discernment and understanding from above establish my path as well as for the woman joining me for this journey. May the name of Jesus be lifted high.

Amen.

SHOWING HOSPITALITY

"Do not forget to show hospitality to strangers, for by so doing some people have shown hospitality to angels without knowing it."

Hebrews 13:2

Lord,

You provided a place for my family's feet to land, turning our four walls into a true home. We have what we need plus some. Thank You for being our true provider. The welcome mat lays outside our front door, a beacon to passersby and those who find their way to our stoop. I desire to welcome others the way You've welcomed us—whether it's inside our home or while we're out and about. I don't want to be so focused on "us" that I forget to offer hospitality. Cause me to notice and take action, Lord.

You are the hospitable God, welcoming me to Your home through the saving grace of Jesus Christ. Your patience and kindness overflow. Your provision overwhelms me. Your notice of my need astounds, oh God. Equip me to extend a similar kindness and love and to take notice of need. Soften my heart so that hospitality pours out of my words and actions to those inside my home and people I meet throughout my day. For Your glory.

Amen.

ARISE NEXT GENERATION

"Consider well her ramparts, view her citadels,
that you may tell of them to the next generation."

Psalm 48:13

Lord,

I watch the world churn in turmoil as society continues to bend a knee to sin. Darkness reaches for the young ones. My concern grows for my children—for the following generations, too. These are my people—names chalked up to the same lineage as me. Will they know You and walk solidly in faith? How can I stand by and not prepare the way with prayer? How can I not fight for them now? Arm me for this battle.

Place the words on my tongue, heavenly Father, to speak life over them. Fill me with a desire to pray without ceasing for their salvation, wisdom, love, and hope. Lead me to share about You in creative ways from morning to night. Your Word details the wrath of sin from nearly the beginning, so there's nothing new—except Your mercies. They're new every morning. May the next generation welcome and know those mercies, walking in a bolder faith than the ones before them. May the next generations rise up and may You call them blessed as You have me.

Amen.

FREEDOM FROM NEGATIVE SELF-TALK

"I praise you because I am fearfully and wonderfully made; your works are wonderful, I know that full well."

Psalm 139:14

Lord,

Your Word tells me I'm fearfully and wonderfully made (Psalm 139:14). I want to believe—and a part of me does—but the chatter in my head skews the story. I lean an ear to its rhetoric. Internal whispers assure that I'm not good enough. The bashing cycles. I wouldn't dare heap these notions on others, though, so why do I allow them to sabotage me? After all, Your hands formed me, and what You make is good. Lord, I need You. Soak me in Your truth and rescue me from negative self-talk.

You created the earth and everything in it. You give orders to the morning and show dawn its place (Job 38:12). Who am I to question Your work? Forgive me, Lord. I praise You because I am fearfully and wonderfully made. Strengthen me to take thoughts captive and squelch my pride. Remind me that You know every hair on my head. You birth within me a righteous view of self. Because of You, I am enough as a woman and a wife. Praise You.

Amen.

Then Caleb silenced the people
before Moses and said,
"We should go up and take
possession of the land,
for we can certainly do it."

Numbers 13:30

AS WE TRAVEL

"The LORD himself goes before you and will be with you;
he will never leave you nor forsake you.
Do not be afraid; do not be discouraged."

Deuteronomy 31:8

Lord,

Once we get to the new destination, we'll hit the ground running, and I'll find the effort worth it. But mid-travel, I often let crankiness set in. I worry that we won't make our flight, I envision breakdowns or a sickness along the way, and I'm concerned we will outspend our allotment. All of this weighs on me, but I know I should entrust it to You. Please help me, Lord.

Prepare the route for safe travels. Remind me that You are present and You go before my family and me. You'll not forsake or leave me today or as my crew and I make our way with new orders in hand. Counsel me with Your wisdom, Holy Spirit. May that wisdom resemble an ocean in our thoughts as my husband and I make decisions concerning routes, flights, and finances. Wash us in Your strength for parenting skills, communication, and health. Praise You, God, that You hold all things together. That You are my true rock and shield.

Amen.

UNITY IN DECISIONS

"Though one may be overpowered, two can defend themselves. A cord of three strands is not quickly broken."

Ecclesiastes 4:12

Lord,

My husband and I face many decisions. You know the subject matter: new orders, living quarters, church, expenses, parenting, retirement, his family and mine, activities, holidays, and so much more. Most of the time, we stand unified with each other and You, but sometimes discord slips in between us. Ease lulls us into giving final say without the input of the other, the kids plot us against each other to obtain a favorable result, or selfishness moves one forward in a decision without consulting the other. Danger lurks in those spaces, though, Lord. Help unify my husband and me.

Check my heart, Lord. Uncover and remove selfish motives. Fill me, instead, with a generous dose of love, wisdom, and selflessness. Fill my husband similarly. Your righteousness helps us make unified decisions—for this military life, our marriage, parenting, finances, and in every day-to-day aspect. You strengthen our bond with a chord of three. You help us navigate unity with success when we cling to Your love, grace, mercy, and righteousness. Thank You. Be glorified, almighty One.

Amen.

WHEN I'M LONELY

"When you pass through the waters, I will be with you; and when you pass through the rivers, they will not sweep over you."

Isaiah 43:2a

Lord,

I'm grateful for this military lifestyle and the blessing of many good friendships. You've blessed me in many ways. You know me, though. Nothing remains hidden from You. With hubby gone, communication sparse, and new orders in hand, loneliness washes over me. Daily, the heaviness builds. And it's hard, so I run to You, for You never leave me. Help me to fend off the isolation that tries to rob me of joy. Remind me that You are with me.

You plucked me from the grip of hell when I called. You've brought friends alongside me at previous stops. My gratitude overflows. Lead me to the companions You planned for here in this new location—if any are in Your plans. Regardless, You are my strength and shield against the solitude that weighs so heavily. You walk with me, and I rejoice. You overflow my days with life, love, and goodness. You fill the space loneliness attempts to occupy—whether it's with Your presence alone or a new friendship. Praise You, almighty God.

Amen.

WHEN GOD GOES SILENT

"Whether you turn to the right or to the left, your ears will hear a voice behind you, saying, 'This is the way; walk in it.'"

Isaiah 30:21

Lord,

When You speak, I hold Your words close. I love the sound of Your voice, whether "hearing" through a stand-out Bible verse, an inner knowing, or another's words that strike a chord of understanding. My heart hums with joy when I hear You. Lately, though, a deafening silence looms. I wonder why You seem distant. Lord, I desire to sense Your instruction and wisdom again. Help me hear You.

Speak to me, Holy One. I long to discern Your voice more clearly and more often. Open my ears and soften my heart. Forgive my sins. I call to You and know that You notice. Draw me closer. Tell me great and hidden things I have not known (Jeremiah 33:3), for You, Great Shepherd, know and lead me. You assure me that I know Your voice. And I do. My heart settles with peace and understanding. I've heard You before and will again. For You are a God who speaks, and I, Your servant, listen. Praise be to You, my God.

Amen.

RUSHING GOD

"For the revelation awaits an appointed time;
it speaks of the end and will not prove false. Though it linger,
wait for it; it will certainly come and will not delay."

Habakkuk 2:3

Lord,

You make and know the plans You have for me, and they ring of goodness and mercy. Sometimes, though, I tire of the wait. I walk in obedience, but as the steps progress, I wonder when You'll act or move. I find difficulty waiting for the appointed time and rush things as if I'm god. Forgive me for this impatience and doubt, Lord. Draw me, for You alone are God. Instill in me a new measure of trust and patience to wait on you.

I release this grip of control. My times are in You, oh Lord. If I tarry here until heaven with dreams left unfulfilled, so be it. Settle my focus on Your plans and goodness, not my strength and perception of timing. You have made everything beautiful in its time. You have placed eternity into man's heart (Ecclesiastes 3:11), and I can trust You with all of mine. You give me courage and strength for the wait. Thank You, heavenly Father.

Amen.

"Amazing grace!
how sweet the sound
That saved a wretch like me!
I once was lost,
but now am found,
Was blind, but now I see."

John Newton,
"Amazing Grace"

BEARING SPIRITUAL FRUIT

"But the fruit of the Spirit is love, joy, peace, forbearance, kindness, goodness, faithfulness, gentleness and self-control. Against such things there is no law."

Galatians 5:22-23

Lord,

I desire to see the fruit of Your Spirit released through me. Godless surroundings and sin's temptation push back at its growth, however. My own struggles sometimes cause me to wonder if love, joy, and other fruits have exited the scene. It's impossible to bear a harvest in small or abundant amounts on my own. To bear good and lasting spiritual fruit, I need You.

Enrich the soil of my heart, Lord. Cause my faith to grow and spiritual goodness to fruit. Bring to blossom and into season an overflowing harvest of love, joy, peace, patience, kindness, goodness, faithfulness, gentleness, and self-control. Prune the temptation, my own selfish desires, and that which fights against godliness. Holy Spirit, sweeten the lives of others with this deliciousness, too—my husband, kids, neighbors, and even strangers I encounter. You help me bear fruit in keeping with repentance (Matthew 3:8), and without You, I can do nothing of spiritual substance. Today, I choose to remain in You, Father, and praise You for the harvest.

Amen.

HIS HEALTH

"Dear friend, I pray that you may enjoy
good health and that all may go well with you,
even as your soul is getting along well."

3 John 1:2

Lord,

I love my husband. Lately, though, his health concerns me. Military work often beats on the body, and my husband has been in the crosshairs. I'm concerned about the harm brewing in his body. Worry knocks at my door. I know I shouldn't let it in, but my thoughts park on whether or not he'll be okay for the long haul. Will we complete this military journey or face a medical discharge earlier than expected? Lord, protect my husband's health, and calm my fears, too.

Restore what's been stolen, and heal him, my loving Savior. May all go well with my husband, and may he enjoy good health. Most importantly, highlight his life as a testimony to You. May his face shine for Your glory. Cast off any anxiety or fear that attempts to infiltrate his thoughts or mine. Fill him with wisdom for nutrition, activity, and medical advice. Top that with the great peace that comes only from above. Thank You for being the Great Physician and his true help.

Amen.

MY HEALTH

"When Jesus saw him lying there and learned that he had been in this condition for a long time, he asked him, 'Do you want to get well?'"

John 5:6

Lord,

With the fluid schedule and lifestyle the military feeds us, it's easy to sweep my health needs aside. But as the one who keeps the home front running in my husband's absence, this isn't wise. To help things flow smoothly at home and to honor my God, I bring my mental, spiritual, and physical health to You.

Disclose any areas ripe for healing within me—whether physically, mentally, or spiritually. Make me well, Jesus. Protect my brain with Your peace. Help me think clearly to make solid decisions. Strengthen my mental health against anxiety, worry, depression, and other attacks. Holy Spirit, my body is Your temple (1 Corinthians 6:19). Send health through these bones, muscles, and the rest of my body. Give me great discernment for wise eating, exercise, and thinking habits. Physical training is of some value, but godliness holds value for all things (1 Timothy 4:8). Above all, loving Father, protect my heart, for You've created this wellspring of life (Proverbs 4:23).

Amen.

WHEN THE WOMB'S EMPTY

"I trust in you; do not let me be put to shame,
nor let my enemies triumph over me."

Psalm 25:2

Lord,

Children surround us. The other military spouses don the title of Mom. But not me. You know how much I wish this womb of mine cradled a child and how many times I've petitioned You with this desire. Yet, our extra bedrooms remain empty, and it hurts. I hear the children out on the sidewalk—their laughter and playful screams rising into the air. It's hard. Surround me and muffle the voice of hurt. Keep my heart in tune with Yours.

Seal off the badgering thoughts of self-protection. Silence the foe. Comfort my grief in a way that only You can. Strengthen me to continue uttering prayers, holding hope in You regardless of the outcome. Bring forth praise and thanksgiving from my lips—for my husband, our marriage, and even the neighborhood children. Lord, I continue to set my prayer before You concerning this, but if I remain childless, bolster my trust in You so that hope doesn't grow dim. Whatever comes, I shall still trust in You, for You are God my Savior. Praise You.

Amen.

GRIEVING ALONE

"Blessed are those who mourn,
for they will be comforted."

Matthew 5:4

Lord,

My heart beats heavy today. Death's aftermath crushes me. Here I sit miles from my loved one who died and from the family surrounding them, wallowing through the murky waters of grief. This is one part of the military lifestyle I could do without—being apart in tough times. How am I going to bear this weight of grief? Alone, it seems impossible. But all's not lost with You. Lord, comfort me, please.

Wrap me in Your love. Cause my thoughts and body to seek out and find peace once again, because You are the God of all comfort. Diminish distance's effect, and comfort my family, for You span the miles. Where's death's sting? Not in Your Kingdom, and I'm grateful. You assure me with heaven and hope. You are the God who sees, and You know how to love me through this. You know my heart and the hurt that beats inside of me. I am comforted by knowing You are here with me and that You've set a plan in motion for eternity. Thank You, Jesus. Your hope brings me solace.

Amen.

BALANCING RELATIONSHIPS WELL

"For I am the LORD your God who takes hold of your right hand and says to you, Do not fear; I will help you."

Isaiah 41:13

Lord,

People and activities slurp up my energy, often leaving little space for my husband or You. If I'm not careful, who I decide to spend time with will tilt the fine balance of relationships unfavorably. I don't want my friends to gather more of my attention than my husband receives. Excess focus on the kids births problems, too. And life's busyness steals away quiet moments from You, Lord. None is good. Show me how to balance relationships well.

Settle within me a yearning to focus on and seek You first, loving Father. Show me how to love You with all of my heart, soul, mind, and strength (Luke 10:27). Rush to my aid concerning scheduling. Lead me to allot and balance time well between my husband and friends, prioritizing him. Pour into me Your wisdom so that I do my part to help keep our relationship rich for the long haul, for my true help comes from above. Thank You for always leading me triumphantly, even in this.

Amen.

I am the Alpha
and the Omega,
the First and the Last,
the Beginning
and the End.

Revelation 22:13

ABOUT THE AUTHOR

Kristi Woods tells stories about God, everyday folks, and a few pretend people through Christian Romance and Christian nonfiction. Mostly, though, she's a Jesus girl. She and her family survived a nomadic military lifestyle and have set roots in Oklahoma, where she keeps a close watch for tornadoes and good chocolate. Find Kristi, faith-building resources, and her recent book releases at *KristiWoods.net.*